C. Knapp

KINGS
OF
ISRAEL

C. Knapp

KINGS
OF
ISRAEL

Kings of Israel

C. Knapp

Published by:
    ECS Ministries
    PO Box 1028
    Dubuque, IA 52004-1028
    phone: (563) 585-2070
    email: ecsorders@ecsministries.org
    website: www.ecsministries.org

First Edition 1909
Revised 2004
Reprinted 2014 (AK '08), 3 Units
Reprinted 2019 (AK '08), 3 Units

ISBN 10: 1-59387-009-4
ISBN 13: 978-1-59387-009-6

Code: B-KOI

Copyright © 2004 ECS Ministries

Originally published as part of a combined volume: *Kings of Judah and Israel*

All Scripture quotations, unless otherwise indicated, are taken from the King James Version of the Bible.

Scripture quotation indicated N.Tr. are from John Nelson Darby's translation of the Old Testament.

Printed in the United States of America

CONTENTS

THE REIGNS OF SAUL, DAVID AND SOLOMON: AN INTRODUCTION BY H. A. IRONSIDE

n complying with the request of the author for an introduction to his truly practical commentary on the books of Kings and Chronicles, I shall attempt to briefly summarize the histories of the three kings of the undivided monarchy, and that only so far as they are set before us in Kings and Chronicles. The lives of Saul and David are much more fully revealed in the books of Samuel, but others have written at length on them as there portrayed, and their writings are still available.

Chronicles opens with the genealogies of the children of Israel, tracing the chosen race right back to Adam. With his name the record begins and, so far as nature is concerned, every name that follows is but another addition of the first man. "The second man is the Lord from heaven." For His coming the world was yet waiting. However, God was indeed quickening souls from the first. There can be no doubt that Adam had obtained divine life when he took God at His word. Accepting the declaration made to the serpent about the seed of the woman (Genesis 3:15), he called his wife's name Eve, "Living," believing that God had found a way to avert the terrible doom their sin had justly deserved. In believing that first gospel message Adam exercised faith; where there is faith, there is of necessity eternal life, and thus a new nature. In many of his offspring, therefore, the same blessed truth is present. And so through these lists, which God has seen fit to preserve and which will be forever kept on high, we see in some the fruit of the new life revealed to the glory of Him who gave it.

There is something intensely solemn in being permitted to go over such a record of names long forgotten by man, but every one of which God has remembered, with every detail of their pathway through this world. Some day our names likewise will be lost to mankind, but neither we nor our ways will be forgotten by God.

Esau's race, as well as that of Israel, is kept in mind; a race from which came mighty kings and princes before any king reigned over Israel (1 Chronicles 1:43). For "that was not first which is spiritual, but that which is natural; and afterward that which is spiritual" (1 Corinthians 15:46). Then, too, some in Israel are only remembered because of some fearful sin that was their ruin, and often the ruin of those associated with them. Those such as Er, and Achan the troubler of Israel (called here Achar), Reuben, who defiled his father's bed, and the heads of the half tribe of Manasseh, who "went a whoring after the gods of the people of the land."

On the other hand, it is sweet and edifying to the soul to notice the brief comments which, if this were a human book, would seem so out of place in the midst of long lists of names. What divine grace had been demonstrated as they trod their oftentimes lowly ways, with faith in exercise and the conscience active. Of this character is the lovely passage about Jabez, who was more honorable than his brethren because he set the Lord before him. His prayer tells of the longings of his soul: "Oh that thou wouldest bless me indeed, and enlarge my coast, and that thy hand might be with me, and that thou wouldest keep me from evil, that it may not grieve me!" We do not wonder when we read that "God granted him that which he requested" (1 Chronicles 4:9–10). The sons of Reuben and their allies who overcame the Hagarites are cited as another instance of the power of faith when "they cried to God in the battle, and he was entreated of them, because they put their trust in him," (5:18–20). Nor does God forget Zelophehad, the man who had no sons to inherit after him, but who claimed a portion for his daughters, and learned that the strength of the Lord is made perfect in weakness (7:15).

There are precious lessons too of an illustrative nature that become evident as we patiently search this portion of the word of the Lord. Who can fail to see the lesson of "the potters, and those that dwelt among plants and hedges: there they dwelt with the king for his work" (4:23)? Surely this represents all who seek to care for the tender plants of the Lord's garden, as well as those who minister to hardier Christians that constitute the hedges. It is only as the servants dwell with the King that they are fit to carry on His work (4:23). The lesson of 1 Chronicles 9:26–34 is similar.

Saul's genealogy begins with 1 Chronicles 8:33, but his whole life is passed over in silence, and only his lamentable end recorded in chapter 10. He it was of whom God said, "I gave them a king in mine anger, and took him away in my wrath" (Hosea 13:11). It was a desire to be like the nations that led Israel to ask for a king; in giving them their request the Lord sent leanness into their souls. Saul was the man of the people's choice, but he was a dreadful disappointment. His dishonored death is on a par with his unhappy life, which is only hinted at in the closing verses of 1 Chronicles 10. All the sorrowful details have been left on record in the books bearing Samuel's name—the prophet who loved him so dearly, but who could not lead him in the ways of God. As another has well described Saul, he was "the man after the flesh." This tells the whole story. In all his life he seemed to have never truly been brought into the presence of God. His activities were all of the flesh, and his way of looking at things was only according to man, and the garish light of man's day. Defeated on Mount Gilboa, he finally committed suicide, and after his death became the laughingstock of the enemies of the Lord.

> So Saul died for his transgression which he committed against the Lord, even against the word of the Lord, which he kept not, and also for asking counsel of one that had a familiar spirit, to enquire of it; And enquired not of the Lord: therefore he slew him, and turned the kingdom unto David the son of Jesse (10:13–14).

Upon the fall of the people's choice, God's man appears on the scene. There is no mention here of the early experiences of David, except that the mighty men are those who went down to the rock to him when he was in the cave of Adullam, and others also who came to him when he was at Ziklag (1 Chronicles 12:1).

The account here given begins with the coming of all Israel to David at Hebron to make him king (1 Chronicles 11). The seven year reign over Judah is not mentioned. Acknowledged by the whole nation as God's appointed ruler, he begins at once the work of enlarging Israel's borders and delivering them from their enemies. Jebus, the fortress of the Jebusites, is taken and converted into the city of David, where he reigns in power, growing greater and greater, thus demonstrating the fact that the Lord of hosts was with him. The mighty men who had shared his rejection are now the sharers of his power and glory. It is a picture of the true David, God's beloved Son, who is yet to be presented in authority over all the earth. Then those who now cleave to Him in humility will be exalted with Him when He takes His great power and reigns.

The ark is brought up to the city of David, but only after the lesson has been learned that God will be sanctified in them that draw close to Him. We learn that, though Philistine carts may do for those who know not the mind of God, where His word is given it must be searched and obeyed. Great are the rejoicings of the people when the symbol of the covenant of the Lord is installed in the place prepared for it, and burnt sacrifices and peace offerings ascend in a cloud of fragrance to God (1 Chronicles 15–16). But when the king would build a house for the God of Israel, though encouraged by the prophet Nathan in his pious purpose, both king and prophet had to learn that the thoughts of God are above the thoughts of the best and most devoted men. Nathan has to inform him that it cannot be for him to build the house, because he has been a man of blood. When David's son is established in peace on the throne, he will build the house, and all will be in keeping with the times. David then is seen to picture the establishment of the kingdom through the destruction of the enemies of the Lord, while Solomon depicts the reign of peace that is to follow for the thousand years. Bowing in obedience to the word of the Lord, David begins to prepare for the work of the temple by gathering in abundance all the materials that he is able to obtain.

But it is made evident that the ideal King has not yet come. Before he resigns his crown to his son, failure is found in the man after God's own heart. His personal sin, which left so dreadful a blot on his character, is omitted in 1 Chronicles, as befits the character of the book. But his official failure in numbering the people is told in all faithfulness, as also the fact that it was Satan who provoked him to act as he did. But in amazing grace God overrules all to make David's sin the means of showing the site for the future temple of the Lord (1 Chronicles 21). Finally, having set all in order, and arranged even the courses of the priests and Levites who are to officiate in the glorious house of Jehovah, the aged monarch appointed Solomon, his son through Bathsheba, to be king in his stead. After solemnly instructing him both about the kingdom and the house that is to be built, "he died in a good old age, full of days, riches, and honour: and Solomon his son reigned in his stead" (29:28).

In the opening chapters of 1 Kings we see that his last days were not all bright. His failure to properly control his household brought him much sorrow, and embittered his cup when he was too feeble to exert himself as he would have desired. Adonijah's effort to secure the crown for himself resulted in disaster, and eventually in his own death, and Solomon's title is indisputably established.

Solomon's reign begins most auspiciously. He went to Gibeon, where the altar still remained with the tabernacle, to offer sacrifice. God appeared to him in the night with the wondrous message, "Ask what I shall give thee" (1 Kings 3:5). It was as though He placed all His resources at the disposal of faith. The young king prayed for wisdom and

knowledge in order that he may care for the flock committed to him. It was a most remarkable prayer for one placed in
his position, and the Lord displayed His pleasure by confer-
ring on him exceeding abundantly above all that he asked or
thought. His wisdom, celebrated to this day, was admired by
his people and the surrounding nations wherever his fame
was carried.

The main part of the chapters devoted to Solomon, in
both Kings and Chronicles, is occupied with the account of
the temple, every part of which was to depict the glory of
the One greater than Solomon who was yet to come. The
symbolism of this magnificent structure has been discussed at
length by others, and would not properly belong in this introduction. At the dedication of the temple, which had gone
up so silently, Jehovah entered in a manner that none might
misunderstand, and took possession of the house as His own.
Solomon's prayer on that occasion is prophetic of the sad history later recorded in these books. He seemed to see all that
his people would yet have to pass through.

But light and gift are not sufficient of themselves to keep
one in step with God. For a time all goes well with Solomon.
His power is unprecedented. His fame is carried into all lands
penetrated by the trader's caravan or touched by the ship of
the voyager. The queen of Sheba comes from the uttermost
parts of the earth to prove him with hard questions concerning the name of the Lord. She goes away with every question
answered and her heart swelling with the glorious things that
she has both seen and heard. The king's knowledge in all
matters seems to be limitless. "And all the earth sought to
Solomon, to hear his wisdom, which God had put into his
heart" (1 Kings 10:24). It is sad that so glorious a record had
to be blotted by the account of failure that the book of Kings
records, but which is passed over in Chronicles.

"But King Solomon loved many strange women ... when Solomon was old, his wives turned away his heart after other gods" (1 Kings 11:1,4). Such is the terrible fall of the man who was the most privileged of all the rulers that history, sacred or secular, records. He failed to keep his own heart. The Lord lost the place He had once had, and the result was that Solomon sinned grievously after all he had known and enjoyed of the things of God. Idolatry was established in the sight of the holy temple of the Lord. God was dishonored by the man who, above all, had received the most from Him. What a warning to everyone who has experienced His grace! May reader and writer lay it to heart!

As a result of Solomon's sins the Lord stirred up adversaries against him, and in the days of his son tore the kingdom from the house of David, with the exception of the two tribes. The rest of this book will consider this period more fully.

We would only add a few remarks to trace the roots of the division that took place at the death of Solomon. The kingdom was torn in two, never to be reunited until the day of Israel's regeneration still to come, when "the envy also of Ephraim shall depart...Ephraim shall not envy Judah, and Judah shall not vex Ephraim" (Isaiah 11:13).

As descendants of Joseph, who (in Jacob's and Moses' blessings) was exalted above and "separate from his brethren," Ephraim seems ever to have aspired to leadership in the nation. During the time of the Judges, Ephraim's pride had twice broken out in an arrogant manner. After the mighty victory of Gideon's little band over the Midianites that had invaded and ravaged the land, the men of Ephraim sharply criticized Gideon because he had not called them to the war—envying the fame of such a victory. Gideon's gracious answer to their boastful criticism averted a catastrophe (Judges 8:1–3). But their still more conceited rebuke of Jephthah on a later occasion brought upon Ephraim a terrible, though deserved, retribution (12:1–6).

When the Theocracy (God's direct rule in Israel) gave place to the kingdom by Israel's irreverent request, Saul, taken from "little Benjamin," is acclaimed by all Israel. Benjamin having been nearly annihilated for their sin some time before, and being Joseph's full brother, may for that reason have been more welcome to Ephraim. But when David, of the tribe of Judah, was revealed as God's anointed in the place of rejected Saul, and at Saul's death was made king in Hebron by Judah, he is not acclaimed. He was opposed by the other tribes, of whom Ephraim was chief, and a seven-year war followed. When the weak pretender of Saul's house (Ish-Bosheth) fell before the rising power of David and Judah, Israel is reunited in one kingdom under David's godly and righteous rule. The jealousy and strife that broke out on previous occasions is for the time forgotten and out of sight.

David's sin, and his son's wicked conduct, brought about upheavals in the kingdom. Later on, Solomon's departure from God and oppression of His people, caused them, at his death, to make demands on the new king Rehoboam. His insolent and foolish answer brings about the crisis in which the unthankful and heartless cry is heard, "What portion have we in David? neither have we inheritance in the son of Jesse: to your tents, O Israel! now see to thine own house, David" (1 Kings 12:16). Ephraim, headed by Jeroboam—an Ephraimite—then takes leadership of the ten tribes that had revolted from the house of David. Thereby a new kingdom is formed, in which every one in the line of their nineteen kings is an apostate from Jehovah.

I now leave the reader with what my beloved fellow servant has penned, praying that he may have your anointed eye and submissive heart, which alone makes the truth living and real in the soul.

AUTHOR'S
INTRODUCTION

t is the author's purpose in this volume to review briefly the histories of the kings of Israel, as recorded in the inspired books of the Kings and Chronicles. These histories are given to us in more or less detail, and do not read exactly the same in each book. God has surely a purpose in this, and it is the glory of saints to search out these matters and to discover, if possible, why these differences exist. There can be no contradiction for "there is one Spirit," and He who inspired the historian of the Kings also controlled and directed the writer of the Chronicles.

These two historical books of the Old Testament bear a relation to each other somewhat similar to that existing between the four Gospels of the New Testament. In the gospels we have a quartet of evangelical biographers, all giving glimpses of the Lord's life, no two in just the same way. They did not even record any single event of that marvelous life of God incarnate in the same way; nor did they report verbatim any discourse of the divine Master. The evangelists Matthew, Mark, Luke, and John are like the four parts in some sublime musical composition. Each part differs from the other, yet together they form a most perfect harmony because they are arranged by one master musician. Each part is perfect in itself, yet requires the others to give the intended fullness. The one part expresses sweetness; the other, strength; another, pathos; and still another, profundity. Each part is essential to the proper expression of the other three and in the combination of the four we have the full, grand harmony. So the four Gospels, though differing, are all the compositions of one author—the Holy Spirit. Each is perfect, yet requires what the others contain to give to the fourfold record the surpassing beauty that every anointed eye beholds in the four evangelists. Each record, being perfectly proportioned to the others, produces that sublime anthem of praise to Heaven's beloved One of whom they speak.

And He was *the* King. In the two books into which we are about to glance we have kings—some comparatively good, and others exceedingly bad; some who made fair beginnings, and foul endings; others who commenced badly, but made a good finish. All, however, came short of God's glory and the divine ideal of what a king should be. He who was, according to the expectation of the Gentile magi, "born King of the Jews," and to the Jew Nathanael "the King of Israel," fulfilled that ideal perfectly. So He is called by Jehovah "My King." And in the fast-approaching day of His kingdom and power He will be known and acknowledged as King of nations (see Matthew 2:2; John 1:49; Psalm 2:6; Revelation 15:3).

Let us now look at the real differences between the Kings and Chronicles, and their significance.

In the LXX (Septuagint) 1 and 2 Kings are called "The third and fourth of the Kingdoms." Originally, in the Hebrew, they were one book like 1 and 2 Samuel. In the *Numerical Bible* Grant wrote, "Samuel and Kings, as we name them, should be, however, as they were originally, but one book each" (volume II, Page 287). The opening word of 1 Kings, Now, indicates that it is really a continuation of Samuel. The history recorded in 1 and 2 Kings is carried on past the middle of the captivity, and ends with Jehoiachin restored to liberty, and his throne set above that of the other kings that were in Babylon—a beautiful, though perhaps faint, shadow of Israel's restoration and exaltation in the coming millennial day. This, as someone has said, is "in happy consonance with its design." It is as "the first ray of God's returning favor," a slight pledge that David's seed and kingdom would (as God said), in spite of past failure, endure forever. Fausset said, in reference to Kings relation to Chronicles, "The language of Kings bears traces of an earlier date. Chaldee forms are rare in Kings, numerous in Chronicles, which has also Persicisms not found in Kings."

The writer of the books of the Kings is not known. The Talmud ascribes it to Jeremiah, which seems somewhat unlikely since the thirty-seventh year of Jehoiachin (the last date in the book) would be sixty-six years after his call to the prophetic office. Besides, the prophet probably died in Egypt with God's rebellious people, whom he so deeply loved and served. On the other hand, as Fausset stated, "The absence of mention of Jeremiah in Kings, though he was so prominent in the reigns of the last four kings, is just what we might expect if Jeremiah be the author of Kings." He remarks further: "In favor of Jeremiah's authorship is the fact that certain words are used only in Kings and in Jeremiah: *baqubuqu,* cruse (1 Kings 14:3; Jeremiah 19:1, 10); *yagab,* husbandman

(2 Kings 25:12; Jeremiah 52:16); *chabah,* hide (1 Kings 22:25; Jeremiah 49:10); *avar,* to bind (2 Kings 25:7; Jeremiah 39:7)."

But whoever the inspired penman may have been, he evidently wrote with a different purpose in view than the author of the Chronicles, who was probably Ezra, the priest. Two names, Akkub and Talmon, found in 1 Chronicles 9:17–18, and mentioned in Nehemiah 12:25–26 as being porters "in the days of Nehemiah, and of Ezra the priest," and Zer-ubba-bel's name with that of others in 1 Chronicles 3:19, prove the writer lived and wrote after the restoration. The fact that the close of Chronicles and opening of Ezra overlap indicates one common author—as Luke and the Acts. Both 1 Chronicles 29:7 and Ezra 2:69 mention the Persian coin *daric* (dram). "The high priest's genealogy is given in the descending line, ending with the captivity, in 1 Chronicles 6:1–15. In Ezra 7:1–5, in the ascending line from Ezra himself to Aaron is given, abridged by the omission of many links, as the writer in Chronicles had already given a complete register" (Fausset). So if a *prophet* (Jeremiah) wrote the Kings, and a *priest* (Ezra) wrote the Chronicles, it would readily account for the ministry of the prophets being so prominent in the former book, and of the priests and Levites in the latter. It might also furnish the key as to the meaning of the marked differences in many portions of the two records.

1 and 2 Chronicles, like Samuel and Kings, were originally one book. They are called in the LXX *Paraleipomena,* or "Supplements". In Hebrew they are called "Words," or "Acts of Days." Its real history (after the genealogies) begins with the overthrow of Saul (1 Chronicles 10), and reads, almost word for word, like the concluding chapter of 1 Samuel, with this marked difference: Saul's body is mentioned in 1 Samuel 31:10 whereas in 1 Chronicles 10:10 his *head* alone is spoken of. In Chronicles there is also a comment on the cause of his

death, not found in Samuel, which would appear to indicate
the author's desire to point out moral lessons in his "supplements" (1 Chronicles 10:13–14). These practical reflections
are frequent in Chronicles; in Kings they rarely occur.

There are other marked differences between the two
books, and all in perfect keeping with the design of each—
divergent, though not contradictory—historian. Let us note
a few of the most prominent. Second Samuel 24:24 says
"David bought the threshingfloor [of Araunah] and the oxen
for fifty shekels of silver"; 1 Chronicles 21:25 says, "David
gave to Ornan for the place [not the threshing-floor and oxen
merely] six hundred shekels of gold by weight." The molten
sea made by Solomon, 1 Kings 7:26 says, "contained two
thousand baths." Second Chronicles 4:5 says "it received and
held three thousand baths" (its capacity). Frequently Chronicles has "God" where Kings has "Lord" (see 2 Samuel 5:19–
25; 1 Chronicles 14:10–16; 2 Samuel 7:3–4; 1 Chronicles 17:2–
3, etc.). "House of God" is found seven times in Chronicles;
in Kings, not once. In 1 Chronicles 14:3 there is no mention
of David's concubines, as in 2 Samuel 5:13. Nor does Chronicles mention his sin with Bathsheba, nor his son Amnon's
crime against Tamar, nor Absalom's rebellion, nor Sheba's revolt. The idolatries of Solomon and some of the early kings
of Judah are less detailed in Chronicles than in Kings; Chronicles, in fact, scarcely hints at Solomon's sin. Nor does it mention his somewhat questionable act of offering incense "upon
the altar that was before the Lord" (1 Kings 9:5). Hezekiah's
failure, too, is only briefly touched on in Chronicles. Yet we
must not think that there was any attempt made on the part
of the writer of Chronicles to pass over, or wink at, the sins
of the house of David. He records Hanani's reproof of Asa, on
which Kings is silent; also, Jehoram's murder of his brethren,
and his idolatry. Nor does Kings mention Joash's apostasy and

murder of Zechariah, Amaziah's sin of idolatry, nor Uzziah's sin of sacrilege. On the other hand, the refreshing account of Manasseh's repentance is peculiar to Chronicles; yet no mention is made in that book of the liberation of the captive Jehoiachin.

Kings gives only seven verses to Uzziah's reign, and but five to righteous Jotham's. Chronicles, on the other hand, summarizes Jehoiakim's reign in four verses, and Jehoiachin's in two. Israel is in the background in Chronicles; Judah and Jerusalem are (with the priests and Levites) its principal subject. However in Kings, Israel and her prophets (as Ahijah, Elijah, Elisha, Jonah, etc.), are prominent.

Another marked distinction between these two interesting books is the sources from which their writers obtained their material. In Kings it is evidently always derived from state records such as "the book of the acts of Solomon" (1 Kings 11:41); "the book of the chronicles of the kings of Judah" (1 Kings 14:29); "the book of the chronicles of the kings of Israel" (1 Kings 14:19), etc. Chronicles embodies more the writings of (or selections from) individuals such as "Samuel the seer," "Nathan the prophet," "Gad the seer," "the prophecy of Ahijah the Shilonite," "the visions of Iddo the seer," "the book of Shemaiah the prophet," "the story of the prophet Iddo," "the book of Jehu the son of Hanani," "Isaiah the prophet," etc. (1 Chronicles 29:29; 2 Chronicles 9:29; 12:15; 13:22; 20:34; 26:22).

The explanation of all this seems to be that the author of Kings wrote his book in Judah, where he would have access to the national archives; while the writer of Chronicles probably compiled his histories from the above-mentioned prophetical writings that were carried with the exiles to Babylon, or obtained after their restoration to the land. This would make the Chronicles peculiarly the book of the remnant;

while the Kings would be more for the nation at large, par-
ticularly Israel. And if this be so, it would explain why the sins
of the earlier kings are veiled in Chronicles, and those of
some of the later ones detailed. Being under Gentile domination, the Israelites were more or less in communication
with them, and in all probability they would come in contact
with these records of the Hebrew kings. Their later history
would be better known to Gentiles, and it would be well for
them to know just why they were permitted to destroy
Jerusalem and hold the nation in bondage; hence the record
of the sins of Josiah, Amaziah, Uzziah, and others. There was
no need to record the sins of David, Solomon, and their immediate successors, as this did not in any way concern the
Gentiles. It was probably in view of Gentile readers that *God*
is so frequently used in Chronicles, instead of His covenant
name *Jehovah,* that they might know that He is "not the God
of the Jews only, but of the Gentiles also." This reaching out
to the Gentiles is the branches of the blessing of Joseph beginning to hang over the wall (Genesis 49:22). Also perhaps
this is the reason for the genealogical record given in 1 Chronicles 1 where we read of some people who are not of Israel,
but all extending back to Adam, common father of us all.
Note, too, in view of this, Asa's crushing defeat of Zerah the
Ethiopian, recorded only in Chronicles, and his reproof by
the prophet for relying on the king of Syria; Jehoshaphat's
triumph over the vast allied forces of Moab and Ammon;
God's (not *Jehovah's*) helping Uzziah against the Philistines,
Arabians, and Mehunims, and the Ammonites giving him
gifts; Jotham's victory over the Ammonites, and their tribute
of silver, and wheat, and barley, rendered to him; and Manasseh's repentance (that the Gentiles might know God's grace)
—all peculiar to Chronicles. On the other hand, Hezekiah's
weakness in first yielding to, and afterward rebelling against,

Sennacherib (2 Kings 18) is carefully excluded from Chronicles. God never needlessly exposes the faults of His servants to the stranger. "Tell it not in Gath, publish it not in the streets of Askelon," is His beautiful principle of action in such cases.

Then as to Kings, the sins of the house of David in its earlier history are faithfully and minutely recorded, that both Judah and Israel (for whose reading the book was primarily intended) might know the reason for their debased and divided condition. The book gives mainly the history of the northern kingdom, and it is delightful to see that though the terrible sins of its rulers are exposed, any acts of grace or goodness on the part of them or the people are also carefully recorded (see 2 Kings 6:8–23, etc.). Prophets were prominent among the Israelites because they had cut themselves off from the ministry of the priests and Levites (which naturally connected itself with the temple at Jerusalem), and God made merciful provision for their spiritual needs by the prophetic ministry of such men as Elijah, etc.

These, I believe, are the real differences between the Kings and Chronicles. They are by no means so easily defined as those existing between the four Evangelists, and I do not profess to explain all of the many and marked variations that have been pointed out. The differences that have been offered in the foregoing may not be entirely satisfactory to all, but if they afford the reader any real help or clue to further discoveries in this direction, the author's main object will have been accomplished. What both writer and reader most need in these studies is to be more in touch with that blessed Master who, in the midst of His disciples, "opened their understanding, that they might understand the Scriptures."

Before closing this Introduction, it might be well to say a word about the authenticity of these books of Kings and

Chronicles. As to the first, our Lord stamped it with His divine authority by referring repeatedly to it, as in the cases of the widow of Sarepta and Naaman the Syrian. Paul referred to Elijah's intercession against Israel, and James mentioned his earnest prayer in connection with drought and rain. Hebrews 11:35 alludes to the raising of the Shunammite's son; and Jezebel is mentioned by our Lord in Revelation 2:20. Christ stamped the book of Chronicles with the seal of inspiration by alluding to the queen of Sheba's visit to King Solomon, and the martyrdom of Zechariah, "slain between the temple and the altar" (Matthew 23:35).

The histories as given in these books are likewise confirmed by both Egyptian and Assyrian monumental records; Rehoboam being mentioned on Syrian monuments, and Omri, Jehu, Menahem, Hoshea, and Hezekiah in the inscriptions on the monuments of the Assyrian Tiglath-pileser, Sargon, Sennacherib, and Esarhaddon. But Scripture, like its great subject, Christ, neither receives nor requires "testimony from men." The monuments do not prove Scripture to be true; it is only proved, when they agree with the Bible, that *they* are true, and not lies. As we read God's word, "we believe and are sure," because "holy men of God," who wrote these records, "spake as they were moved by the Holy Ghost" (2 Peter 1: 21). True, God's Word is called "prophecy" in that verse, but it has been aptly said that "*history* as written by the prophets is retroverted *prophecy.*" "Moses and the Prophets" (like "the Law and the Prophets") means the Pentateuch, the Old Testament historical books, and the writings generally designated as "the Prophets." And "the prophecy came not in old time by the will of man." So we unhesitatingly declare ourselves, like Paul of old, as "believing *all* things which are written in the law and in the prophets" (Acts 24:14).

CHRONOLOGICAL TABLE

*T*he following is a listing of the kings of Israel subsequent to the reigns of Saul, David, and Solomon, each of which lasted forty years (1051 B.C. to 931 B.C.).

B.C.	KING	LENGTH OF REIGN IN YEARS
931	Jeroboam I	22
910	Nadab	2
909	Baasha	24
886	Elah	2
885	Zimri	Seven days
885	Omri	12
874	Ahab	22
853	Ahaziah	2
852	Jehoram	12
841	Jehu	28
814	Jehoahaz	17
798	Jehoash	16
793	Jeroboam II	41
753	Zachariah	Six months
752	Shallum	One month
752	Menahem	10
742	Pekahiah	2
742	Pekah	20
		(years counted from 752)
732	Hoshea	9
722		Samaria taken

DYNASTIES OF THE KINGS OF ISRAEL

1. Jeroboam; Nadab
2. Baasha; Elah
3. Zimri
4. Omri; Ahab; Ahaziah; Joram
5. Jehu; Jehoahaz; Jehoash; Jeroboam II; Zachariah
6. Shallum
7. Menahem; Pekaiah
8. Pekah
9. Hoshea

JEROBOAM I

Whose people is many
(1 Kings 11:26–40; 12–14:20; 2 Chronicles 10; 13:1–20)

CONTEMPORARY PROPHETS: Ahijah, The Man of God out of
Judah, The Old Prophet of Bethel

The memory of the just is blessed: but the name of the wicked
shall rot.

Proverbs 10:7

Jeroboam is an example of what is not at all uncommon in the East—a man exalted from a comparatively low station in private or public life to the highest, or one of the highest, positions in the land. We have Scriptural examples of this, such as Joseph, and Moses; and secular history mentions not a few. Let us see how Jeroboam's elevation came about:

> And Jeroboam the son of Nebat, an Ephrathite of Zereda,
> Solomon's servant, whose mother's name was Zeruah, a wid-
> ow woman, even he lifted up his hand against the king. And
> this was the cause that he lifted up his hand against the king:
> Solomon built Millo [LXX, 'the citadel'], and repaired the
> breaches of the city of David his father. And the man Jer-
> oboam was a mighty man of valor: and Solomon seeing the
> young man that he was industrious, he made him ruler over all
> the charge [or, levy] of the house of Joseph [that is, Ephraim
> and Manasseh] (1 Kings 11:26–28).

This naturally gave him a place of importance in the eyes
of his fellow countrymen, and prepared the way for what was
soon to follow. They evidently resented this enforced labor.
"Thy father," they afterwards said to Rehoboam, "made our
yoke grievous." They spoke of it too as a heavy yoke (1 Kings
12:4). There is no certain evidence that this was really so.
What was being done by their labor was for the glory and security of the kingdom, whose prosperity would profit all (see
1 Kings 4:25). It is possible, however, that they were set to
work on what served only for self-gratification; for when
men depart from the right way, as Solomon did, they soon
become oppressive. This would furnish some justification for
their discontent, which Jeroboam would take no pains to al-
lay. He probably had discernment sufficient to see how final
circumstances were gradually shaping themselves, and had his
own personal ambitions in mind, as shall be presently seen.

> And it came to pass at that time when Jeroboam went out of
> Jerusalem, that the prophet Ahijah the Shilonite found him in
> the way; and he had clad himself with a new garment; and

they two were alone in the field. And Ahijah caught the new garment that was on him, and rent it in twelve pieces: And he said to Jeroboam, Take thee ten pieces: for thus saith the Lord, the God of Israel, Behold, I will rend the kingdom out of the hand of Solomon, and will give ten tribes to thee…because that they have forsaken me, and have worshiped Ashtoreth the goddess of the Zidonians, Chemosh the god of the Moabites, and Milcom the god of the children of Ammon, and have not walked in my ways, to do that which is right in mine eyes, and to keep my statutes and my judgments, as did David his father…And it shall be, if thou wilt hearken unto all that I command thee, and wilt walk in my ways, and do that is right in my sight, to keep my statutes and my commandments, as David my servant did; that I will be with thee, and build thee a sure house, as I built for David, and will give Israel unto thee (1 Kings 11:29–38).

It was a solemn word, to which Jeroboam ought to have given earnest heed. Had he done so, he would never have come to his own melancholy end, nor would his dynasty have been so suddenly and violently terminated—before the second generation had barely begun.

Whether news of Ahijah's prophecy reached the ears of Solomon, or the elated Jeroboam betrayed the secret by some overt act of rashness or insubordination, we are not told. But we read, "Solomon sought therefore to kill Jeroboam. And Jeroboam arose, and fled into Egypt, unto Shishak king of Egypt, and was in Egypt until the death of Solomon." In 1 Kings 11:26 we read, "He lifted up his hand against the king." Jeroboam may have led some abortive attempt to raise a rebellion, perhaps to hasten the fulfillment of the prophecy concerning him (compare 2 Samuel 20:21). How unlike David, the man after God's own heart, who would not injure a hair of the condemned king's head, or raise a finger to bring the kingdom to himself even though he had been anointed and chosen by the prophet Samuel to supersede Saul! David was a man of faith; and faith—that precious gift of God—ever waits on God for His time and way to fulfill His promises.

But Jeroboam knew nothing of faith. He had aspired secretly after power over his brethren, as the expression, "according to all that thy soul desireth," clearly shows (1 Kings 11:37). He probably sought the fulfillment of Ahijah's prophecy with pride's feverish haste, therefor he was compelled to seek an asylum in Egypt, under the protection of Shishak. This king had but recently overthrown the late dynasty with which Solomon had unlawfully allied himself by marriage. Ahijah had distinctly said that Solomon would be "prince all the days of his life," and it was only out of his son's hand that the kingdom would be taken and transferred to Jeroboam. But like a willful, impatient child, he could not wait, and took the case out of God's hand to undertake for himself.

How long Jeroboam remained in Egypt is not known; but we read that on the death of Solomon he returned and was present at Rehoboam's coronation, when the rebellion was consummated. "And Rehoboam went to Shechem: for all Israel were come to Shechem to make him king. . . . And Jeroboam and all the congregation of Israel came, and spake unto Rehoboam." The time was ripe. Solomon's incompetent son and successor, instead of heeding his father's wholesome proverb, "A soft answer turneth away wrath: but grievous words stir up anger," displayed his lack of wisdom and fitness to govern a liberty-loving people. As a consequence, he precipitated the separation of the already alienated northern tribes. Rehoboam weakened and almost ruined a kingdom that had but recently extended from the Nile to the Euphrates, a distance of more than 450 miles, acknowledged by the surrounding nations as one of the most powerful empires of the earth.

The details of that memorable schism need not be entered into here, (see chapter on Rehoboam in the companion volume *Kings of Judah*.) We have dwelt on the cause from the human or circumstantial side chiefly; the divine side is also given: "Wherefore the king [Rehoboam] hearkened not unto the people; for the cause was from the Lord, that he might perform his saying, which the Lord spake by Ahijah the Shilonite unto Jeroboam the son of Nebat" (1 Kings 12:15).

Jeroboam became the spokesman of the disaffected tribes in the presentation of their petition, whose rejection snapped the already overstrained link that bound the tribes together. Though only presenting the people's petition, it is nevertheless probable that Jeroboam was not idle, but like an artful politician, busy behind the scenes until the coveted crown became his: "And it came to pass, when all Israel heard that Jeroboam was come again, that they sent and called him unto the congregation, and made him king over all Israel" (1 Kings 12:20). He made historic Shechem his capital, and fortified it. He also made Penuel an important strategic point. *Penuel* means "the face of God," which should have reminded him of God's past dealings with the scheming Jacob (Genesis 32:31). Someone described Shechem: "The situation is lovely; the valley runs west, with a soil of rich, black vegetable mould, watered by fountains, sending forth numerous streams, flowing west: orchards of fruit, olive groves, gardens of vegetables, and verdure on all sides, delight the eye"—the very spot for a man bent on self-pleasing, and aspiring to a life of luxury.

But the newly crowned king quickly manifested that he did not hold his kingdom in faith as a trust from God. "And Jeroboam said in his heart, Now shall the kingdom return to the house of David" (the all-seeing eye of God reveals what was going on in his heart, which had never been anything but an evil heart of unbelief). He continued, "if this people go up to do sacrifice in the house of the Lord at Jerusalem, then shall the heart of this people turn again unto their lord, even unto Rehoboam king of Judah, and they shall kill me, and go again to Rehoboam king of Judah." "As a man thinketh in his heart, so is he." This man had neither trust in God, nor confidence in his fellows. He was like former king Saul who, departing from God, began to be suspicious of everybody around him. Jeroboam evidently felt that he had no real hold on the people's affections, and that his tenure of the crown was very precarious. He therefore wickedly devised a plan (which, sadly, proved all too successful) to prevent a return of the tribes to their former allegiance to the house of David.

> Whereupon the king took counsel, and made two calves of gold, and said unto them, It is too much for you to go up to Jerusalem: behold thy gods, O Israel, which brought thee up out of the land of Egypt. And he set the one in Bethel, and the other put he in Dan (1 Kings 12:28–29).

The old limits of the land were from Dan to Beersheba. Bethel lay near the southern border of Jeroboam's kingdom, and about twelve miles north of Jerusalem; while Dan was in the far north, at the sources of the Jordan. Thus by placing the calves at these extreme limits of his dominion, with the pretext of giving all an easy access to a place of worship, the uneasy king hoped to prevent their return to Judah's God and kingdom. His kingdom, unlike Judah with its temple at Jerusalem, had no divine center. In fact, it was a circumference without a center, and its worship a matter of convenience and expediency.

"And this thing became a sin: for the people went to worship before the one, even unto Dan" (Bethel was taken from Jeroboam by Abijah; see 2 Chronicles 13:19). "And he made a house of high places, and made priests of the lowest of the people, which were not of the sons of Levi." This was a direct violation of the law of God in reference to the priesthood (see Numbers 18:1–7). And he did not stop there; he evidently regarded the legitimate priests and the Levites with special suspicion and rejected their services. "For Jeroboam and his sons had cast them off from executing the priest's office unto the Lord: and he ordained him priests for the high places, and for the devils, and for the calves which he had made" (2 Chronicles 11:14–15). Abijah, in his speech before the battle with Jeroboam, said to him and his followers,

> Have ye not cast out the priests of the Lord, the sons of Aaron, and the Levites, and have made you priests after the manner of the nations of other lands? so that whosoever cometh to consecrate himself with a young bullock and seven rams, the same may be a priest of them that are no gods (2 Chronicles 13:9).

The error of the organized church, Protestant and Catholic, is the assumption of all priestly functions by a humanly consecrated few, to the exclusion of every member of the church, every one of which is a priest, according to the testimony of Scripture (see 1 Peter 2:5,9). The priesthood of believers is not a continuation or an amplification of the Jewish priesthood, but one of an entirely different order—"a royal priesthood." Christ is the great High Priest of whom Aaron was the type, and every true believer a priest of the same spiritual family, typified by Aaron's sons. Hebrews 5:4 has its direct application to the high priesthood only, though the principle may be applied to ministry; but to Christian priesthood proper the verse has no application whatever, for a believer is a priest, not by special call, but solely by virtue of his link with Christ by faith.

Lessons from Jeroboam's act as to the priesthood can surely be learned by both Catholicism and Protestantism, but the right of a class among God's people to the exclusive exercise of priestly or ministerial functions is certainly not one of them. On the contrary, his action illustrates just what these groups have done—shutting out the body of those who are truly the children of God, and therefore truly priests, and consecrating to the office men who have never been born of God, and have no right or qualification whatever therefore to the privilege.

Viewed even as a stroke of policy, this ejection of the Lord's priests and the Levites was a blunder. Almost all of them went over to Jeroboam's rival, and thereby strengthened the kingdom of Judah. By being overly anxious to preserve his power, he lost what was no doubt the choice part of his kingdom. Similar to this was the banishment of the Huguenots from France—the most intelligent, enterprising and God-fearing portion of its citizens—an act from which that country has never yet fully recovered, and perhaps never will. The Netherlands and other parts of the Continent suffered the same in the persecution of those of the Reformed persuasion. And in England none were more faithful and true than those stalwart sons who for conscience' sake forsook the land they loved, and sought an asylum among the desolate wildernesses of America.

Other unlawful innovations were introduced by Jeroboam.

So he offered upon the altar which he had made in Bethel the fifteenth day of the eighth month, even in the month which he had devised of his own heart; and ordained a feast unto the children of Israel: and he offered upon the altar, and burnt incense (1 Kings 12:33).

This feast of Jeroboam's was in imitation of the feast of tabernacles, which God had commanded to be observed in the *seventh* month: the eighth was the month which Jeroboam "had devised of his own heart"—always deceitful and desperately wicked. How many practices and customs in Christendom have been devised of men's own hearts and have no foundation in Scripture! For many seem to imagine that it is quite permissible in spiritual things to do "every man that which is right in his own eyes," instead of "Thus saith the Lord." God condemned Israel for doing that which He said, "I commanded them not, neither came it into my heart" or "mind" (Jeremiah 7:31; also, 19:5; 32:35). It is the thoughts of *God's* heart, not mine, that I am to heed and put into practice. These He has revealed in His Word, and it is our happiness and wisdom to heed *that,* and not the commandments and doctrines of men.

"And, behold, there came a man of God out of Judah by the word of the Lord unto Bethel: and Jeroboam stood by the altar to burn incense." If Jeroboam would not have Jehovah's *priests,* God sends His *prophet* into his land.

And he cried against the altar in the word of the Lord, and said, O altar, altar, thus saith the Lord: Behold, a child shall be born unto the house of David, Josiah by name; and upon thee shall he offer the priests of the high places that burn incense upon thee, and men's bones shall be burnt upon thee. And he gave a sign the same day, saying, This is the sign which the Lord hath spoken; Behold, the altar shall be rent, and the ashes that are upon it shall be poured out (1 Kings 13:1–3).

It was a bold message, but delivered in faithfulness. It was directed not against the king, but the priests, though the king seemed to feel the force of its application to himself.

> And it came to pass, when king Jeroboam heard the saying of the man of God, which had cried against the altar in Bethel, that he put forth his hand from the altar, saying, Lay hold on him. And his hand, which he put forth against him, dried up, so that he could not pull it in again to him. The altar also was rent, and the ashes poured out from the altar, according to the sign which the man of God had given by the word of the Lord (4–5).

Jeroboam had forgotten, or ignored, the reproof administered by God to kings almost a thousand years before; "Touch not mine anointed, and do my prophets no harm" (Psalm 105:14–15). He was quickly reminded of his error, and entreated pardon. "And the king answered and said unto the man of God, Entreat now the face of the Lord thy God, and pray for me, that my hand may be restored me again." But it was his *heart* that had need of healing, rather than his hand. In this he was like the mass of men today, who look more to the hand and its deeds than the heart of sin that prompted the evil acts. The penitent publican struck his breast, as if to express that there, from within, came all the transgression, iniquity, and sin.

However Jeroboam was in a measure humbled, and his appeal for the prophet's intercession was regarded: "And the man of God besought the Lord, and the king's hand was restored him again, and became as it was before." He who would have persecuted the prophet, now would entertain and give him a reward for his healing. "And the king said unto the man of God, Come home with me, and refresh thyself, and I will give thee a reward." But, like Daniel, who nobly answered king Belshazzar, "Let thy gifts be to thyself, and give thy rewards to another" (Daniel 5:17), so also the man of God refused to be patronized (take note, all ye servants of the living God), saying,

> If thou wilt give me half thy house, I will not go in with thee, neither will I eat bread nor drink water in this place: for so it was charged me by the word of the Lord, saying, Eat no bread, nor drink water, nor turn again by the same way that thou camest. So he went another way, and returned not by the way that he came to Bethel (1 Kings 13:8–10).

It is not our purpose to follow the history of the man of God, who was seduced to his death by the lie of the apostate old prophet of Bethel (1 Kings 13:11–32). But the narrative is full of wholesome instruction for us all, to adhere strictly to the word of God and not be beguiled away from the simple path of obedience by the deceptions of men, professed "prophets" though they be; yea, be it an angel from Heaven even, "let him be accursed" that perverts or contradicts the word of God. This history should be pondered by all for like all things written in God's Word, it was written for our warning and instruction.

Jeroboam gained no lasting lesson from the prophet's faithful testimony, or the mercy shown him in the restoration of his withered hand, for we read, "After this thing [the prophet's death?] Jeroboam returned not from his evil way, but made again of the lowest of the people priests of the high places: whosoever would, he consecrated him, and he became one of the priests of the high places. And this thing became sin unto the house of Jeroboam, even to cut it off, and to destroy it from off the face of the earth" (1 Kings

13:33–34).

The threatened destruction of Jeroboam's house now begins.

> At that time Abijah the son of Jeroboam fell sick. And Jeroboam said to his wife, Arise, I pray thee, and disguise thyself, that thou be not known to be the wife of Jeroboam; and get thee to Shiloh: behold, there is Ahijah the prophet, which told me that I should be king over this people. And take with thee ten loaves, and cracknels, and a cruse of honey, and go to him: he shall tell thee what shall become of the child (1 Kings 14:1–3).

Jeroboam's troubled spirit did not turn to the old prophet of Bethel, or to others like him in Israel, but in his distress he turned to Jehovah's prophet—a not uncommon thing with sinners. This is a striking witness of the power of conscience, as well as a testimony to the influence of a righteous man in the midst of abounding evil. Ashamed probably to have it known among his subjects that he preferred to consult a prophet of Jehovah before those of his own idolatrous system, Jeroboam sent his wife in disguise; or since Shiloh with Bethel and other neighboring towns had been taken by Abijah king of Judah (see 2 Chronicles 13:19), she would be entering enemy territory. Or could it be that, conscious of guilt and afraid of bad news, he hoped to deceive the prophet? Whatever his reason, Jeroboam's wife complied with her husband's command.

> And the Lord said unto Ahijah, Behold, the wife of Jeroboam cometh to ask a thing of thee for her son; for he is sick: thus and thus shalt thou say unto her: for it shall be, when she cometh in, that she shall feign herself to be another woman.

And it was so, when Ahijah heard the sound of her feet, as she came in at the door, that he said, Come in, thou wife of Jeroboam; why feignest thou thyself to be another? for I am sent to thee with heavy tidings. Go, tell Jeroboam, Thus saith the Lord God of Israel, Forasmuch as I exalted thee from among the people, and made thee prince over my people Israel, and rent the kingdom away from the house of David, and gave it thee: and yet thou hast not been as my servant David, who kept my commandments, and who followed me with all his heart, to do that only which was right in mine eyes; but thou hast done evil above all that were before thee: for thou hast gone and made thee other gods, and molten images, to provoke me to anger, and hast cast me behind thy back. Therefore, behold, I will bring evil upon the house of Jeroboam, and will cut off from Jeroboam every male, and him that is shut up and left in Israel, and will take away the remnant of the house of Jeroboam, as a man taketh away dung, till it be all gone. Him that dieth of Jeroboam in the city shall the dogs eat; and him that dieth in the field shall the fowls of the air eat: for the Lord hath spoken it. Arise thou therefore, get thee to thine own house: and when thy feet enter into the city, the child shall die. And all Israel shall mourn for him, and bury him: for he only of Jeroboam shall come to the grave, because in him there is found some good thing toward the Lord God of Israel in the house of Jeroboam (1 Kings 14:5–13).

Heavy tidings these were indeed to a mother's heart! She was possibly a good woman, to have a son in whom God saw "some good thing toward the Lord." Sad indeed must have been her journey back to the city and her dwelling, on entering which her son would die! "And Jeroboam's wife arose, and departed, and came to Tirzah: and when she came to the threshold of the door, the child died; and they buried him;

and all Israel mourned for him. according to the word of the Lord, which he spake by the hand of his servant Ahijah the prophet." *Abijah* ("Jehovah is my Father") was his name; and his heavenly Father called him home. It was an instance of the righteous being "taken away from the evil to come." And it is written, "He shall enter into peace: they shall rest in their beds, each one walking in his uprightness" (Isaiah 57:1–2). We shall expect to meet and greet thee, Jehovah's little child, in that bright morning when for those who have part in the first resurrection there shall be no more evil to come.

Jeroboam's battle with king Abijah, and his crushing defeat, have been entered into elsewhere (see ABIJAH, *Kings of Judah*), so need not be repeated here. Both the battle and his child's death must have occurred toward the close of his reign (see 2 Chronicles 13:1). Thus disaster and sorrow would combine to help hasten his end; and we read, "Neither did Jeroboam recover strength again in the days of Abijah: and the Lord struck him, and he died." God chastened him through two Abijahs; one of his own house, and the other of the house of David—terribly significant to him who had cast that same Jehovah behind his back.

"And the rest of the acts of Jeroboam, how he warred, and how he reigned, behold, they are written in the book of the chronicles of the kings of Israel." This is that Jeroboam who "drave Israel from following the Lord, and made them sin a great sin" (2 Kings 17:21). God has placed the stamp of eternal infamy on his name.

NADAB

Willing
(1 Kings 15:25–31)

The house of the wicked shall be overthrown:
but the tabernacle of the upright shall flourish.
Proverbs 14:11

*A*nd Nadab the son of Jeroboam began to reign over Israel in the second year of Asa king of Judah, and reigned over Israel two years. And he did evil in the sight of the Lord and walked in the way of his father, and in his sin wherewith he made Israel to sin."

The sons of Jeroboam, together with their father, had rejected God's ordained priesthood, and had "cast them off from executing the priest's office unto the Lord" (2 Chronicles 11:14). So Nadab followed in his father's ways; but God did not permit him to continue long in his wickedness. "And Baasha the son of Ahijah, of the house of Issachar, conspired against him; and Baasha smote him at Gibbethon, which belonged to the Philistines; for Nadab and all Israel laid siege to Gibbethon" (1 Kings 15:27).

Gibbethon was a town in Dan, allotted to the Levites of the family of Korah (Joshua 19:44; 21:23). It bordered on the land of the Philistines, and was probably seized by them on the emigration of the Levites to Judah. *Gibbethon* means "lofty place," and it was while seeking to recover it to the crown, that Nadab was treacherously slain. But it was in fulfillment of the prophecy of Ahijah, "The Lord shall raise him up a king over Israel, who shall cut off the house of Jeroboam that day: but what? even now" (1 Kings 14:14).

"In the third year of Asa king of Judah did Baasha slay him, and reigned in his stead" (1 Kings 15:28). Once on the throne, Baasha began to execute the judgment of Jehovah against the remaining members of the house of Jeroboam, according to the aged Ahijah's word.

And it came to pass, when he reigned, that he smote all the house of Jeroboam; he left not to Jeroboam any that breathed, until he had destroyed him, according unto the saying of the Lord, which he spake by his servant Ahijah the Shilonite: because of the sins of Jeroboam which he sinned, and which he made Israel sin, by his provocation wherewith he provoked the Lord God of Israel to anger.

So ended the first of the nine dynasties that for 250 years ruled (or misruled) the kingdom of Israel. Nadab's name means "willing," and he appears to have been too willing to continue in and perpetuate the sin of his iniquitous father. He is not once mentioned in the book of Chronicles, nor is there any record in that book of his father's lifting up his hand against king Solomon, as in the Kings. The inspired record of his uninteresting reign ends with the usual formula used in Kings: "Now the rest of the acts of Nadab, and all that he did, are they not written in the book of the chronicles of the kings of Israel?"

BAASHA

He who seeks, or lays waste
(1 Kings 15:27–16:7; 2 Chronicles 16:1–6)

CONTEMPORARY PROPHET: Jehu son of Hanani

The Lord hath made all things for himself: yea, even the wicked
for the day of evil.

Proverbs 16:4

In the third year of Asa king of Judah began Baasha
the son of Ahijah to reign over all Israel in Tirzah, twenty and
four years." With the beginning of a new dynasty, and the sad
history of that which had been before him, one might hope
that Baasha would have taken a different course, and turned
to Jehovah. Alas, we read: "And he did evil in the sight of the
Lord, and walked in the way of Jeroboam, and in his sin

wherewith he made Israel to sin" (1 Kings 15:33–34).

He was of Issachar, and had the tribal characteristic—an eye for what appeared pleasant (Genesis 49:15). So he made beautiful Tirzah (which some derive from *ratzah,* "pleasant"; see Song of Solomon 6:4) the royal residence during his reign. Whatever he may have known of God's *purpose* in the cutting off of Jeroboam's house, his *motive* was not one of righteousness (like Jehu's, later), for he was no better than those he murdered, and continued to walk in their sin.

> Then the word of the Lord came to Jehu the son of Hanani against Baasha, saying, Forasmuch as I exalted thee out of the dust, and made thee prince over my people Israel; and thou hast walked in the way of Jeroboam, and hast made my people Israel to sin, to provoke me to anger with their sins; Behold, I will take away the posterity of Baasha, and the posterity of his house [a terrible thought to an Israelite!] and will make thy house like the house of Jeroboam the son of Nebat. Him that dieth of Baasha in the city shall the dogs eat; and him that di-eth of his in the fields shall the fowls of the air eat (1 Kings 16:1–4).

His doom, and that of all his house, is here solemnly pro-nounced. "Out of the dust" implies Baasha's lowly origin. How often do revolutionists imagine that because the ob-noxious ruler is of noble birth, or royal lineage, the remedy is to put in the place of power one of their own class and rank! And how soon are they made to learn that "a servant when he ruleth" is the very worst type of tyrant known (Proverbs 30:21–22). No, it is not a question of natural birth, whether high or low, but of *new* birth and ruling in the fear of God, which gives to any favored land such sovereigns as "Victoria the Good." Baasha was of plebeian stock, yet his name, "he who lays waste," tells only too accurately what kind of a ruler he proved himself to be.

There was war between Baasha and Asa king of Judah all their days. He made a league with Benhadad king of Syria, and built or fortified Ramah on his southern border to prevent, if possible, the migration of his subjects to Judah, where they were attracted by the prosperity enjoyed under Asa.

"Now the rest of the acts of Baasha, and what he did, and his might, are they not written in the book of the chronicles of the kings of Israel? So Baasha slept with his fathers, and was buried in Tirzah: and Elah his son reigned in his stead." And then a supplementary verse is added to emphasize the fact that it was because of his idolatries and murder of the house of Jeroboam that God judged him and his family:

> And also by the hand of the prophet Jehu the son of Hanani came the word of the Lord against Baasha, and against his house, even for all the evil that he did in the sight of the Lord, in provoking him to anger with the work of his hands [his idols], in being like the house of Jeroboam; and because he killed him (1 Kings 16:5–7).

God, who looks on the heart, saw him but as an assassin for the accomplishment of his ambitious designs, slaying king Nadab and the entire house of Jeroboam.

ELAH

An oak
(1 Kings 16:8–14)

Behold, the righteous shall be recompensed in the earth: much more the wicked and the sinner.

Proverbs 11:31

In the twenty and sixth year of Asa king of Judah began Elah the son of Baasha to reign over Israel in Tirzah, two years. And his servant Zimri, captain of half his chariots, conspired against him, as he was in Tirzah, drinking himself drunk in the house of Arza, steward of his house in Tirzah. And Zimri went in and smote him, and killed him, in the twenty and seventh year of Asa king of Judah, and reigned in his stead."

Of the house of Jeroboam God had said: "I will take away

the remnant of the house of Jeroboam as a man taketh away dung, till it all be gone"—so would it be with Baasha who had removed the remnant of Jeroboam's house by murder. "Drinking himself drunk" was Elah's occupation at the time of his assassination. Dissipation does not appear to have been the special sin of the kings of Israel and Judah generally (nor has it ever been characteristic of the Jewish race), as was the case with so many of their Gentile neighbors—for example, Ben-hadad with his thirty-two confederate kings "drinking himself drunk in the pavilions" (1 Kings 20:16).

Josephus wrote that Elah was slain while his army was away at the siege of Gibbethon, begun in his father Baasha's day (*Antiquities* 8.12.4). His murder was perpetrated in the house of his steward *Arza* ("earthliness"), who was probably as given to self-indulgence as his master (contrast Ahab's steward Obadiah, 1 Kings 18:3).

His murderer Zimri at once began to massacre all the house of Baasha, sparing none of his family or friends. It was complete extermination, even as God had ordained it should be.

> Thus did Zimri destroy all the house of Baasha, according to the word of the Lord, which he spake against Baasha by Jehu the prophet, For all the sins of Baasha, and the sins of Elah his son, by which they...made Israel to sin, in provoking the Lord God of Israel to anger with their vanities [idolatries] (1 Kings 16:12–13).

Thus the house of Baasha, like that of Jeroboam before him, became extinct—to Jewish minds, the greatest calamity that could overtake a man.

In less than fifty years the first two dynasties of Israel's kings had come to an end and every member of their families been exterminated. God meant to make their doom an example to those who would follow their ungodly ways. They stand as beacons, in these records, to warn all rulers and subjects away from the rocks on which these kings were wrecked to their everlasting ruin. "Who is wise, and he shall understand these things? prudent, and he shall know them? for the ways of the Lord are right, and the just shall walk in them: but the transgressors shall fall therein" (Hosea 14:9). The usual formula ends the record of Elah's worthless life (1 Kings 16:14).

ZIMRI

Musical

(1 Kings 16:9–20)

Whoso walketh uprightly shall be saved: but he that is perverse in
his ways shall fall at once.

Proverbs 28:18

      n the twenty and seventh year of Asa king of Judah
did Zimri reign seven days in Tirzah. And the people were
encamped against Gibbethon, which belonged to the Philistines. And the people that were encamped heard say, Zimri
hath conspired, and hath also slain the king: wherefore all
Israel made Omri, the captain of the host, king over Israel
that day in the camp."

    "The triumphing of the wicked is short" (Job 20:5). This
was sharply exemplified in the case of Zimri, who triumphed

just one week. He appears to have had no support from the people, who knew his character and desired not his rule. News of his assumption of the crown had no sooner reached the army at Gibbethon than they rejected his claims by proclaiming their commander-in-chief, Omri, king.

> And Omri went up from Gibbethon, and all Israel with him, and they besieged Tirzah. And it came to pass, when Zimri saw that the city was taken, that he went into the palace of the king's house, and burnt the king's house over him with fire, and died, For his sins which he sinned in doing evil in the sight of the Lord, in walking in the way of Jeroboam, and in his sin which he did, to make Israel to sin (1 Kings 16:17–19).

Murderers are generally desperate characters; and when it is beyond their power any more to destroy the lives of others, they, like wretched Zimri, frequently destroy their own. Satan was a murderer from the beginning, and he knows how to goad them on to their destruction—body and soul. He knows the suicide's destiny after death. We read that Judas, the traitor who committed suicide, went "to his own place" (Acts 1:25)—the place where the unbelieving, the abominable, murderers, and such like, have their place—in the lake of fire (Revelation 21:8).

Zimri's perfidy became a byword in Israel. The infamous Jezebel could refer to him and say, "Had Zimri peace, who slew his master?" (2 Kings 9:31). "Treason is punished by treason," one has said, "and the slayer is slain." In Zimri was fulfilled the true proverb, "A man that doeth violence to the blood of any person shall flee to the pit; let no man stay him" (Proverbs 28:17). Let Zimri's end warn traitors and intentional murderers of kings.

OMRI

Heaping
(1 Kings 16:15–28)

Contemporary Prophet: Elijah (?)

The curse of the Lord is in the house of the wicked: but he blesseth the habitation of the just.

Proverbs 3:33

*C*ivil war, that most deplorable of all forms of armed conflict, followed Omri's assumption of the throne of Israel. We read that "all Israel made Omri, the captain of the host, king over Israel that day *in the camp*"—that is, the *army* that was encamped against Gibbethon. But a part of the tribes championed the cause of Tibni. "Then were the people of Israel divided into two parts: half of the people followed Tibni the son of Ginath, to make him king; and half followed Omri." Omri would be thus, during the four years' contest, in the position of military dictator. And with the soldiery at his command, he could hardly fail to prevail in the end against his adversary, whose death probably put an end to the conflict. Then Omri as king began a new dynasty.

> In the thirty and first year of Asa king of Judah began Omri to reign over Israel, twelve years: six years reigned he in Tirzah. And he bought the hill Samaria of Shemer for two talents of silver, and built on the hill, and called the name of the city which he built, after the name of Shemer, owner of the hill, Samaria [Hebrew: *Shomeron*] (1 Kings 16:23–24).

In the siege of Tirzah, Omri may have seen its undesirability as a capital, from a military standpoint; or the pride of founding a new capital may have led him to choose the hill of Shemer. It lay about six miles to the northwest of Shechem, the old capital. The situation of Shemer, according to Josephus, combined strength, fertility, and beauty. The hill was six hundred feet above the surrounding country, and "the view," one writes, "is charming." But more attractive to the Christian heart, is the site of the old capital, Shechem, near the place where our Lord, "wearied with his journey, sat thus on the well." And there, in the ears of Jacob's erring daughter, He told of the free-giving God and of that living water, which if a man drink, he shall never more thirst (John 4).

"But Omri wrought evil in the eyes of the Lord, and did worse than all that were before him. For he walked in all the way of Jeroboam the son of Nebat, and in his sin wherewith he made Israel to sin, to provoke the Lord God of Israel to anger with their vanities" (idolatries). He seems to have formulated laws making Jeroboam's calf worship or other forms of idolatry obligatory throughout his realm. These laws remained in force until the end of the kingdom, more than two hundred years later. "For the statutes of Omri are kept, and all the works of the house of Ahab"—that is, Baal worship (Micah 6:16). Such yokes men willingly bear and even cling to, so prone is the human heart to idolatry.

Omri was founder of the fourth and most powerful of the Israelite dynasties—combining ability with the establishment of the basest idolatry. He formed an alliance with Ben-hadad I king of Syria, who had streets made for, or assigned to, him in Samaria (see 1 Kings 20:34). Samaria is called on the Assyrian monuments *Beth Omri* ("house of Omri"), in agreement with 1 Kings 16:24. On the black obelisk, however, Jehu is mistakenly called "son of Omri." His name appears on the Dibon stone, on which Mesha states that Omri subjected and oppressed Moab until he, Mesha, delivered them out of his hand.

"Now the rest of the acts of Omri which he did, and his might that he showed, are they not written in the book of the chronicles of the kings of Israel?" He used his might, not to Israel's deliverance, but for the furtherance and establishment of idolatry, to Israel's ruin. His name was common to three tribes, Benjamin, Judah, and Issachar (see 1 Chronicles 7:8; 9:4; 27:18); so it is not certain out of which tribe Omri came— though probably from Issachar (like Baasha). The murderous Athaliah, his granddaughter, is usually linked with his name in Scripture (see 2 Kings 8:26; 2 Chronicles 22:2).

"So Omri slept with his fathers, and was buried in Samaria. And Ahab his son reigned in his stead." *Omri* means "heaping"; by his iniquity he helped to heap up wrath against his dynasty. God executed His indignation 36 years later on his great-grandson Joram, to the total extinction of the guilty house.

AHAB

Brother of [his] father
(1 Kings 16:29–17:1; 18:1–22:40; 2 Chronicles 18)

CONTEMPORARY PROPHETS: Elijah, and Micah son of Imlah

When the wicked are multiplied, transgression increaseth; but the righteous shall see their fall.
Proverbs 29:16

*A*nd in the thirty and eighth year of Asa king of Judah began Ahab the son of Omri to reign over Israel: and Ahab the son of Omri reigned over Israel in Samaria twenty and two years. And Ahab the son of Omri did evil in the sight of the Lord above all that were before him. And it came to pass, as if it had been a light thing for him to walk in the sins of Jeroboam the son of Nebat, that he took to wife Jezebel the daughter of Ethbaal king of the Zidonians, and went and served Baal, and worshipped him. And he reared up an altar for Baal in the house of Baal, which he had built in Samaria."

Ahab was not the first to introduce Baal worship in Israel: it had been known among them since their entrance into the land. But under his rule and the powerful influence of Jezebel, his wife, it became the established form of idolatry, as calf worship was made under Jeroboam. Baal was the sun god of the ancient inhabitants of the land (as of the Phoenicians), and his worship was accompanied by the most obscene rites and impurities.

Dius and Menander, Tyrian historians, mention Ithobalus, a priest of Ashtoreth during Ahab's time. They wrote that Ithobalus murdered Pheles, and became king of Tyre. This was in all probability Jezebel's father. Her zeal for the spread and maintenance of the worship of Baal and Ashtoreth, or Astarte (female consort of Baal), is therefore easily accounted for. It would also explain her inveterate hatred of the holy worship of Jehovah, and her murderous designs against His prophets. Her name means "chaste"—Satan's counterfeit or ridicule, as it were, of purity. Was it the hope of strengthening his kingdom, or her seductions with the attractions of her painted face, that led Ahab into this alliance? Behind it all, we may be sure, Satan was seeking by this new move to utterly corrupt and destroy God's people and His truth from the earth. "And Ahab made a grove"—*Asherah,* an image or pavilion to Astarte—"and Ahab did more to provoke the Lord God of Israel to anger than all the kings of Israel that were before him."

"In his days did Hiel the Bethelite build Jericho: he laid the foundation thereof in Abiram ['father of height'] his firstborn, and set up the gates thereof in his youngest son Segub ['aloft'], according to the word of the Lord, which he spake by Joshua the son of Nun." Jericho properly belonged to Judah. Hiel, instead of remaining at Bethel within his sovereign's realm, presumed to fortify (for this is what *build* means here) the city for his master Ahab, that he might command the channel of Jordan. For this disobedience and disregard of God's word (see Joshua 6:26) the threatened judgment fell on his first and lastborn sons. *Hiel* means, "God liveth," and he discovered to his sorrow that Jehovah was the living God, whose word will stand, and none can transgress it with impunity. Every transgressor, and all "the sons of disobedience," will find that He is always true to His word. "Hath he said, and shall he not do it? or hath he spoken, and shall he not make it good?" (Numbers 23:19) His prophecy concerning Jericho, spoken through Joshua five hundred years before, was fulfilled on the house of Hiel (Joshua 6:26).

But God, who did not wink at Ahab's or the nation's wickedness, would yet seek through discipline to turn them back from their folly, and sent to them His servant Elijah. "And Elijah the Tishbite, who was of the inhabitants of Gilead, said unto Ahab, As the Lord God of Israel liveth, before whom I stand, there shall not be dew nor rain these years, but according to my word" (1 Kings 17:1). Jehovah, not Baal, was Israel's God, in spite of Jezebel's seemingly successful attempt to force her Canaanitish gods on them; and Ahab would be made to know it. God used a millennial form of discipline to teach him this (see Zechariah 14:17). For three and one half years the land lay under the divine condemnation of drought and famine. This drought appears to have extended even to Gentile lands, for it is mentioned in the annals of the Greek historian Menander (Josephus *Antiquities* 8.13.2).

> And it came to pass after many days, that the word of the Lord
> came to Elijah in the third year, saying, Go, show thyself unto
> Ahab; and I will send rain upon the earth....And Ahab called
> Obadiah, which was the governor [steward] of his house.
> (Now Obadiah feared the Lord greatly: For it was so, when
> Jezebel cut off the prophets of the Lord, that Obadiah took a
> hundred prophets, and hid them by fifty in a cave, and fed
> them with bread and water.) And Ahab said unto Obadiah, Go
> into the land, unto all fountains of water, and unto all brooks:
> [perhaps] we may find grass to save the horses and mules alive,
> that we lose not all the beasts (1 Kings 18:1–5).

Ahab, as someone has said, cared more for the beasts of
his stables than for his poor, starving subjects.

One wonders how a man like *Obadiah,* whose name
means "worshiper of Jehovah," came to hold office under
such an abandoned idolater as Ahab. But there were also
saints in Nero's palace, whose salutations were considered
worthy of apostolic mention. Godliness, as has been quaintly
said, "is a hardy plant, that can live amidst the frosts of persecution and the relaxing warmth of a corrupt court, and not
merely in the conservatory of a pious family."

"As Obadiah was in the way," Elijah suddenly appeared
before him, and gave him a terse message for his master: "Go,
tell thy lord, Behold, Elijah is here." The poor lord high
chamberlain, knowing well the murderous character of his
master, trembled for his life.

> He said, What have I sinned, that thou wouldest deliver thy
> servant into the hand of Ahab, to slay me? As the Lord thy God
> liveth, there is no nation or kingdom, whither my lord hath
> not sent to seek thee: and when they said, He is not there; he
> took an oath of the kingdom and nation, that they found thee

not. And now thou sayest, Go, tell thy lord, Behold, Elijah is here. And it shall come to pass, as soon as I am gone from thee, that the Spirit of the Lord shall carry thee whither I know not; and so when I come and tell Ahab, and he cannot find thee, he shall slay me (9–12).

He evidently knew that the husband of Jezebel set little value on any of his subjects' lives, and in his present temper would not hesitate, on the least provocation or suspicion, to slay him without mercy.

Assured by Elijah that Ahab would find him, Obadiah delivered his message. "And Ahab went to meet Elijah. And it came to pass, when Ahab saw Elijah, that Ahab said unto him, Art thou he that troubleth Israel?" What audacity! Elijah answered, "I have not troubled Israel; but thou, and thy father's house, in that ye have forsaken the commandments of the Lord, and thou hast followed Baalim" (or, the Baals).

The prophet then proposed to test publicly on mount Carmel whether Jehovah or Baal were God. To this the king accedes. "So Ahab sent unto all the children of Israel, and gathered the prophets together unto mount Carmel." The test was accordingly made, to the utter discomfiture of the Baal prophets. "Jehovah, He is God! Jehovah, He is God!" all the people cried; and at Elijah's command the four hundred and fifty prophets of Baal are led down to the brook Kishon, and slain there (1 Kings 18).

Since the people once again acknowledged Jehovah as God, and the prophets of Baal were destroyed, the purpose of the drought was accomplished. "And Elijah said unto Ahab, Get thee up, eat and drink; for there is a sound of abundance of rain."

Years later, James called our attention to the prophet's intercessory prayer: "Elijah was a man subject to like passions as we are, and he prayed earnestly that it might not rain: and it rained not on the earth...and he prayed again, and the heavens gave rain" (James 5:17–18). A cloud, "like a man's hand" at first, soon filled the whole sky: the prayer is answered, and in the power of the Spirit of faith Elijah sends the word by his servant, "Go up, say unto Ahab, Prepare thy chariot, and get thee down, that the rain stop thee not. And it came to pass in the mean while, that the heaven was black with clouds and wind, and there was a great rain. And Ahab rode, and went to Jezreel" (1 Kings 18:44–45).

Jezebel's indomitable will is now stirred to passion. Enraged, she threatened with an oath to make Elijah's life like that of her slaughtered priests, and he in fear flees from the kingdom. She was evidently the real ruler in Israel, for Ahab, so far as Scripture informs us, did not make even the mildest kind of protest against her murderous threat.

Ahab's weakness is further demonstrated by his servile answer to the besieging king of Syria:

> And Ben-hadad the king of Syria gathered all his host together: and there were thirty and two kings with him, and horses, and chariots: and he went up and besieged Samaria, and warred against it. And he sent messengers to Ahab king of Israel into the city, and said unto him, Thus saith Ben-hadad, Thy silver and thy gold is mine; thy wives also and thy children, even the goodliest, are mine. And the king of Israel answered and said, My lord, O king, according to thy saying, I am thine, and all that I have (20:1–4).

And when the messengers returned with more insolent demands, the king would probably have submitted to the humiliating conditions proposed, had not his more spirited and patriotic subjects advised otherwise saying, "Hearken not unto him, nor consent." A wicked man is never really any-thing but a *weak* man. It is only "the righteous who are bold as a lion" (Proverbs 28:1). When Ahab refused the king of Syria his unsoldierly demand, he said half apologetically, "This thing I may not do." He did not use the bold, intensive "*will* not" that was used by the three Hebrew children when they were under more helpless circumstances, and to a more powerful king (Daniel 3:18). Angered at even this meekly-put refusal "Ben-hadad sent unto him, and said, The gods do so unto me, and more also, if the dust of Samaria shall suffice for handfuls for all the people that follow me." Then, more nobly, poor Ahab answered: "Tell him, Let not him that gird-eth on his harness boast himself as he that putteth it off." Provoked at this reply, Ben-hadad, under the influence of drink, gave the mad order for instant attack on the city. But God's time for the humiliation of insolent Benhadad had come:

> And, behold, there came a prophet unto Ahab king of Israel, saying, Thus saith the Lord, Hast thou seen all this great multi-tude? behold, I will deliver it into thy hand this day; and thou shalt know that I am the Lord. And Ahab said, By whom? And he said, Thus saith the Lord, Even by the young men [Hebrew: *servants*] of the princes of the provinces. Then he said, Who shall order the battle? And he answered, Thou (1 Kings 20:13–14).

God would humiliate Ben–hadad, not by any show of strength through the seven thousand soldiers left to Ahab, but by the *servants* of the princes of the provinces, who numbered two hundred and thirty-two. "And they went out at noon. But Benhadad was drinking himself drunk in the pavilions, he and the kings"—the thirty-two kings that helped him.

And the young men of the princes of the provinces went out first; and Ben-hadad sent out, and they told him, saying, There are men come out of Samaria. And he said, Whether they be come out for peace, take them alive; or whether they be come out for war, take them alive. So these young men of the princes of the provinces came out of the city, and the army which followed them. And they slew every one his man: and the Syrians fled; and Israel pursued them: and Ben-hadad the king of Syria escaped on a horse with the horsemen. And the king of Israel went out, and smote the horses and chariots, and slew the Syrians with a great slaughter (20:17–21).

The expression "The king of Israel went out," coming as it does after the account of the victory of the young men and the small army, seems to imply that though, according to the prophet's word, Ahab would order the battle, he remained cautiously behind until the rout of the besiegers had begun. Then, when danger was past, he came out from his place of security within the city walls, and assisted in slaughtering an already defeated foe. God gave his army victory, that he might have another proof in addition to that already offered on mount Carmel—so condescending and gracious is He—that He was Jehovah, the unchanging One. Through this victory He would also encourage and foster any little faith that might, as a result of the recent demonstration on mount Carmel, have sprung up in the hearts of the nearly apostate nation. God calls trust in Him "precious faith" (2 Peter 1:1), so highly does He value it. In how many ways does God seek to gain and hold the confidence of men, for their everlasting good and glory! Do you have that precious faith?

"And the prophet came to the king of Israel, and said unto him, Go, strengthen thyself, and mark, and see what thou doest: for at the return of the year the king of Syria will come up against thee." What patient, marvelous grace is God's! His goodness would lead men to repentance. So He sent His prophet, even to Ahab, to warn him of what the Syrians would do. "And it came to pass at the return of the year, that Ben-hadad numbered the Syrians, and went up to Aphek, to fight against Israel." Aphek lay about six miles east of the sea of Galilee, on the direct road between the land of Israel and Damascus, and was a common battlefield of the Syrian kings (see 2 Kings 13:17).

> And the children of Israel were numbered, and were all present, and went against them: and the children of Israel pitched before them like two little flocks of kids; but the Syrians filled the country. And there came a man of God, and spake unto the king of Israel, and said, Thus saith the Lord, *Because the Syrians have said,* The Lord is God of the hills, but He is not God of the valleys, *therefore* will I deliver all this great multitude into thy hand, and *ye shall know that I am Jehovah* [another demonstration that Jehovah was the God of Israel] (1 Kings 20:27–28, italics added).

For a whole week the two hostile armies lay encamped against each other. When they joined battle on the seventh day, the "two little flocks of kids," with God on their side, destroyed a host of a hundred thousand men. And the remnant of the defeated army, numbering twenty-seven thousand, that escaped being slaughtered by those whose land they had invaded without provocation, fled into the city of Aphek where a wall fell on them. The method is unimportant with Israel's God, Jehovah, who is called "the God of battles"; He can save by many or by few. When a mere handful (a few thousand) does not completely destroy a vast army, He can shake down a wall on those who escaped, and thus complete the deserved destruction.

This was the *third* occasion, within a short space of time, on which God would convince the king of Israel and his people that He was what His prophets proclaimed Him to be—Jehovah, the God of Israel. He insists that, among men, "in the mouth of two or three witnesses," every word shall be established; and He will not Himself use an easier rule in His dealings with the sons of men. Ahab had this threefold testimony given him, but he entirely failed to profit by it. He was ensnared by Ben-hadad's guile after God had placed him in his power; he not only let him live, but said, "He is my brother." It was the beginning of his final downfall.

A prophet now, by skillful ingenuity, brings before Ahab what he had done. Having induced a fellow prophet to smite him, so that in smiting he wounded him, he then disguised himself, and hailed the king as he was passing by. "And he said, Thy servant went out into the midst of the battle; and, behold, a man turned aside, and brought a man unto me, and said, Keep this man: if by any means he be missing, then shall thy life be for his life, or else thou shalt pay a talent of silver. And as thy servant was busy here and there, he was gone." Ahab probably thought the beggar appealed to him in fear for his life or the ruinous fine. Then he, like David before, pronounced his own sentence:

> And the king of Israel said unto him, So shall thy judgment be; thyself hast decided it. And he [the prophet] hasted, and took the ashes away from his face; and the king of Israel discerned him that he was of the prophets. And he said unto him, Thus saith the Lord, Because thou hast let go out of thy hand a man whom I appointed to utter destruction, therefore thy life shall go for his life, and thy people for his people. And the king of Israel went to his house heavy and displeased [sullen and

vexed, N.TR.], and came to Samaria (40–43).

He made the same fatal mistake that king Saul made when he spared Agag. His calling the enemy of Israel *my brother* and taking him up into his chariot, may have sounded well and looked liberal to men like himself, who would applaud his conduct as magnanimous; but in God's eyes it was unpardonable disobedience, for which he and the nation would be made to suffer. Men might praise him, but of what worth are human applause to the man whose conduct God condemns? Ahab was not the last of that generation who love "the praise of men more than the praise of God" (John 12:43).

From that time Ahab appears to be given up of God: first, to covetousness and murder, and then to make war with and be slain by that nation whose blaspheming king he had called *my brother* and permitted to escape.

The first, his coveting of Naboth's vineyard, and the false accusation and murder of that righteous man, form one of the most painful and soul-stirring chapters in human history, whether secular or inspired.

> And it came to pass after these things, that Naboth the Jezreelite had a vineyard, which was in Jezreel, hard by the palace of Ahab king of Samaria. And Ahab spake unto Naboth, saying, Give me thy vineyard, that I may have it for a garden of herbs, because it is near unto my house: and I will give thee for it a better vineyard than it; or, if it seem good to thee, I will give thee the worth of it in money (1 Kings 21:1–2).

Naboth fearlessly refused the king's offer and said: "The Lord forbid it me, that I should give the inheritance of my fathers unto thee." This was not obstinacy on Naboth's part, as some have supposed; nor yet a stubborn refusal to surrender his legal rights to do his king a favor. He was contending, not for his own rights (which scarcely becomes one who owes his all to God's free grace), but for God's, and those of his successors. "The land shall not be sold forever," God had said. Merciful provision was made in the law for a man who might have become reduced to extreme poverty. He was permitted to sell the land, but only to the year of jubilee, when it was to revert back to the original owner or his heirs. Naboth could not plead poverty so had no excuse to sell his vineyard, even to the king. There was also a law relating to property within a city's walls, which if sold, must be redeemed within a year, or remain the possession of the purchaser forever (see Leviticus 25). If Naboth's vineyard, adjoining Ahab's palace, lay within the city walls, it would, if sold, pass for all time out of the hands of Naboth's heirs. Be that as it may, his firm refusal to sell out to his royal neighbor was a matter of conscience.

Araunah's sale of his threshing floor to David, and Omri's purchase of the hill of Samaria cannot be called parallel cases. In the first instance Araunah, though a Jebusite (a Gentile), seemed fully to understand David's purpose, and agree with it. It was therefore surrendering and offering his property to the Lord Himself (2 Samuel 24:15–25). In the second, the moral condition of the nation was such that Shemer, an Israelite, was probably unconcerned as to what God had said concerning the disposal of his land (1 Kings 16:24). Naboth was right, both toward God and toward his family ties, whatever his critics may be disposed to say to the contrary. His resolute adherence to the right, cost him both his good name and his life.

"And Ahab came into his house heavy and displeased because of the word which Naboth the Jezreelite had spoken to him: for he had said, I will not give thee the inheritance of my fathers. And he laid him down upon his bed, and turned away his face, and would eat no bread." His petulant conduct was inappropriate for anyone—much less a king; it was rather that of a spoiled child, peevish and in ill humor because thwarted in his desire by one of his subjects.

"But Jezebel his wife came to him, and said unto him, Why is thy spirit so sad, that thou eatest no bread?" Informed as to the cause of his dejection, her daring spirit finds a ready way out of Ahab's difficulty. "And Jezebel his wife said unto him, Dost thou now govern the kingdom of Israel?" Alas, was it not she that governed it really, with more daring ungodliness than Ahab, her puppet husband? "Arise," said she, "and eat bread, and let thy heart be merry. I will give thee the vineyard of Naboth the Jezreelite." Herself the daughter of a Gentile king, she was thoroughly schooled in court methods of disposing of refractory subjects. She had not learned, as David in God's school, that kings should be the *shepherds* of the people. Might made right in the kingdoms of the nations, and she would show her Hebrew husband how quickly Naboth's objections to the king's demands could be overcome, in spite of anything or everything written in the Mosaic code.

So she wrote letters in Ahab's name, and sealed them with his seal, and sent the letters unto the elders and to the nobles that were in his city, dwelling with Naboth. And she wrote in the letters, saying, Proclaim a fast, and set Naboth on high among the people: and set two men, sons of Belial, before him, to bear witness against him, saying, Thou didst blaspheme God and the king. And then carry him out, and stone him, that he may die (1 Kings 21:8–10).

How base could such men be, to lend themselves as willing tools to her perfidious designs, and carry out her instructions to the letter! Yet, public conscience might rebel at open murder, therefore some appearance of justice had to be given her act. Furthermore, the nation may still have been experiencing the moral effect of the events on mount Carmel, so this nefarious patron of Baal had to proceed in her wickedness with a measure of caution. "And the men of his city, even the elders and the nobles who were the inhabitants in his city, did as Jezebel had sent unto them, and as it was written in the letters which she had sent unto them."

Jezebel had had her will, but oh, the dreadfulness of using God's institution to carry out the will of the flesh! She knew the penalty for blasphemy against Jehovah was death (Leviticus 24:16). She would find associates to prove Naboth guilty of this, and thus avenge herself on the man who had dared to say no to the desire of power. But, according to Jewish teachers, if Naboth were found guilty of blasphemy alone, his property would fall to his heirs the same as if he had died under ordinary or natural circumstances. To secure the vineyard, a further charge—one of treason—must be trumped up against him; in such a case the estate of the condemned man went to the royal exchequer. So Naboth was accused of blasphemy both against God and the king (see Exodus 22:28). And when the dark deed was done, the instigator of it coolly sent to her husband saying, "Arise, take possession of the vineyard of Naboth the Jezreelite, which he refused to give thee for money: for Naboth is not alive, but dead. And it came to pass, when Ahab heard that Naboth was dead, that Ahab rose up to go down to the vineyard of Naboth the Jezreelite, to take possession of it" (1 Kings 21:15–16).

But Naboth's God was not dead; He was still the God "that liveth and seeth," as Ahab was soon to know.

And the word of the Lord came to Elijah the Tishbite, saying,
Arise, go down to meet Ahab king of Israel, which is in
Samaria: behold, he is in the vineyard of Naboth, whither he is
gone down to possess it. And thou shalt speak unto him, saying, Thus saith the Lord, Hast thou killed, and also taken possession? And thou shalt speak unto him, saying, Thus saith the
Lord, In the place where dogs licked the blood of Naboth shall
dogs lick thy blood, even thine (17–19).

Like most wicked men when reproved, Ahab considered
the fearless messenger of God as an enemy. "Hast thou found
me, O mine enemy?" he asked. "Is it thou, the troubler of Israel?" he had asked the faithful prophet on a former occasion
(1 Kings 18:17, N.TR.). Here, since he could no longer link
the nation with himself in his guilt, he acknowledged the
personal character of the prophet's ministry, and called him
his (not the nation's) enemy.

And he answered, I have found thee: because thou hast sold
thyself to work evil in the sight of the Lord. Behold, I will
bring evil upon thee, and will take away thy posterity, and will
cut off from Ahab every [male], and him that is shut up and
left in Israel, And will make thy house like the house of Jeroboam the son of Nebat, and like the house of Baasha the son
of Ahijah, for the provocation wherewith thou hast provoked
me to anger, and made Israel to sin (20–22).

Judgment on Jezebel also is then pronounced. "And it
came to pass, when Ahab heard those words, that he rent his
clothes, and put sackcloth upon his flesh, and fasted, and lay
in sackcloth, and went softly." Ahab is really affected, though
superficially no doubt, by the prophet's declaration. God,

who ever approves even the slightest indication of repentance in transgressors, said to Elijah, "Seest thou how Ahab humbleth himself before me? because he humbleth himself before me, I will not bring the evil in his days: but in his son's days will I bring the evil upon his house."

We have now the closing incident in the life of this king of Israel, who "did sell himself to work wickedness in the sight of the Lord, whom Jezebel his wife stirred up."

"And they continued three years without war between Syria and Israel." In the third year, Jehoshaphat king of Judah (now linked to the house of Ahab by the marriage of his son and heir-apparent to the throne, Jehoram, to Athaliah, Ahab's daughter) came down on a friendly visit to the Israelite capital. Ahab saw in the presence of so powerful an ally a splendid opportunity to use him for the extension of his kingdom. So he said to his servants, "Know ye not that Ramoth in Gilead is ours, and we be still, and take it not out of the hand of the king of Syria?" Ramoth-gilead was an important fortress, directly east of Samaria, and about twenty miles back from the Jordan. It was occupied during Solomon's magnificent reign by Ben-Geber, one of his twelve commissariat officers (1 Kings 4:13). Ben-hadad I, had taken it from Omri, according to Josephus (*Antiquities* 8.15.3). On Ahab's proposing to jointly recover this place to their family (now united), Jehoshaphat at once acceded, saying, "I am as thou art." The four hundred court prophets all declared the success of the expedition a foregone conclusion. "Go up," they said unanimously; "for the Lord shall deliver it into the hand of the king" (2 Chronicles 18:5 has "God," instead of "the Lord," as in 1 Kings 22:6: see Author's Introduction). Ahab's ally did not appear entirely satisfied with such offhand, emphatic prophecies of good fortune; he had evidently some misgivings of conscience, and was suspicious of this crowd of state-paid "peace-and-safety" preachers. So he cautiously asked if there was not another of Jehovah's prophets within call, of whom they might further inquire. "There is yet one man," answered Ahab, "Micaiah the son of Imlah, by whom we may inquire of the Lord: but I hate him; for he doth not prophesy good concerning me, but evil." And the good-natured king of Judah, ever willing to interpret in the best way others' deeds or words, replied, "Let not the king say so." "Hasten hither Micaiah the son of Imlah," Ahab commanded his officer.

The two ill-matched kings sat each on his throne, arrayed in his robes of state, in an open space at the entrance of the gate of Samaria. Before them were gathered all the pseudo-prophets, prophesying their lies before their royal master and his uneasy confederate. One of the deceivers, striving after dramatic effect, had made iron horns, saying, "Thus saith the Lord, With these shalt thou push the Syrians, until thou have consumed them." "Go up to Ramoth-gilead, and prosper," they all with one voice said: "for the Lord shall deliver it into the king's hand."

Next the unpopular prophet was unceremoniously brought into the presence of the consulting kings. In ironical agreement with what the time-serving four hundred had been saying, he also said, "Go, and prosper!" Ahab was quick to understand his irony, and adjured him (put him under oath) in Jehovah's name, to tell him nothing but that which was true. "And he said, I saw all Israel scattered upon the hills, as sheep that have not a shepherd: and the Lord said, These have no master: let them return every man to his house in peace." "Did I not tell thee that he would prophesy no good concerning me, but evil?" said Ahab to Jehoshaphat, on hearing this solemn announcement. Jehovah's prophet next sets before them his vision of a scene in Heaven: the lying spirit in the mouth of Ahab's prophets to allure him to his death. But this is more than Ahab can bear, and he orders at once that Micaiah be thrust into prison, and to be fed with the bread and water of affliction until he returned from his expedition in peace. "And Micaiah said, If thou return at all in peace, the Lord hath not spoken by me. And he said, Hearken, O people, every one of you" (1 Kings 22:28).

Could all this take place in the presence of Jehoshaphat, and he not protest? We know not. Scripture is silent here. But sadly, what may not even a child of God stoop to when he is away from God, in evil company!

The two kings now proceed to Ramoth-gilead, and Ahab's treachery and cowardice again appear. He artfully disguised himself, while inducing the unsuspecting Jehoshaphat to appear in battle in his royal robes. Corrupt and contemptible trickery! He protected his own person at the probable sacrifice of his generous friend. But "the unjust knoweth no shame," and living for self destroys all nobleness of character. The unhappy monarch had also been under Jezebel's influence too long to have any honor remaining in him. Besides, he probably feared Micaiah's prophecy more than he believed his own prophets. The Syrians, assuming Jehoshaphat to be the king of Israel, crowded close around him for a time. But God delivered him, and they perceived their mistake. And one of the soldiers drew a bow at random, and smote the king of Israel between the sections of his armor. "Wherefore he said unto the driver of his chariot, Turn thy hand, and carry me out of the host: for I am wounded." And at even, at the time of the going down of the sun, he died; "and the blood ran out of the wound into the midst of the chariot." The day was lost to Israel, and the humiliated army returned leaderless from the ill-fated campaign.

"So the king died, and was brought to Samaria: and they

buried the king in Samaria. And one washed the chariot in the pool of Samaria; and the dogs licked up his blood; and they washed his armor; according unto the word of the Lord which he spake" (37–38). God's arrow found him, in spite of his disguise. And his colleague, though for a time a conspicuous target for every archer in the Syrian army, escaped. How true the couplet, "Not a single shaft can hit, / Till our all-wise God sees fit." None who make God their trust need ever fear "the arrow that flieth by day" (Psalm 91:5).

"Now the rest of the acts of Ahab, and all that he did, and the ivory house which he made, and all the cities that he built, are they not written in the book of the chronicles of the kings of Israel?" He was evidently a man of luxurious tastes, which appears to have been also characteristic of his successors (see Amos 3:15). His moral character, as given in the parenthetic passage of 1 Kings 21:25–26, is a fearfully black one. "But [or surely] there was none like unto Ahab, which did sell himself to work wickedness in the sight of the Lord, whom Jezebel his wife stirred up [Hebrew: *urged on*]. And he did very abominably in following idols, according to all things as did the Amorites, whom the Lord cast out before the children of Israel." As his name means, Ahab was a true "brother (or friend) of his father" Omri, in his excessive wickedness.

The Moabite stone mentions Omri's son; his name also appears on the Assyrian Black Obelisk as "Ahab of Jezreel."

"So Ahab slept with his fathers; and Ahaziah his son reigned in his stead."

AHAZIAH

Whom Jehovah holds
(1 Kings 22:40,49,51–53; 2 Kings 1)

<small>CONTEMPORARY PROPHET:</small> Elijah

The fear of the Lord prolongeth days: but the years of the wicked shall be shortened.

Proverbs 10:27

cripture records a dark catalogue of iniquity concerning Ahaziah. Yet it is only what might be expected of the offspring of such a couple as Ahab and Jezebel. So matched in wickedness were his parents that nothing short of a miracle of grace could have made him anything better than the description given of him here:

Ahaziah the son of Ahab began to reign over Israel in Samaria the seventeenth year of Jehoshaphat king of Judah, and reigned two years over Israel. And he did evil in the sight of the Lord, and walked in the way of his father, and in the way of his mother, and in the way of Jeroboam the son of Nebat, who made Israel to sin. For he served Baal, and worshiped him, and provoked to anger the Lord God of Israel, according to all that his father had done (1 Kings 22:51–53).

"And Ahaziah fell down through a lattice in his upper chamber, that was in Samaria, and was sick: and he sent messengers, and said unto them, Go, enquire of Baal-zebub ['lord of flies'] the god of Ekron, whether I shall recover of this disease." Ekron was the northernmost of the five chief Philistine cities, and contained the shrine and oracle of the vile abomination called Baal-zebub (the Beelzebub of the New Testament). Men love the gods that are most like unto themselves, so it is not surprising to see Ahaziah sending to this miserable Philistine god. But the sick king's messengers never reached the oracle. The God of Israel Himself, sending His prophet to intercept the king's messengers, answered his question.

But the angel of the Lord said to Elijah the Tishbite, Arise, go up to meet the messengers of the king of Samaria, and say unto them, Is it not because there is not a God in Israel, that ye go to enquire of Baal-zebub the god of Ekron? Now, therefore, thus saith the Lord, Thou shalt not come down from that bed on which thou art gone up, but shalt surely die (2 Kings 1:3–4).

The messengers returned to their royal master, and related what had taken place and the prophet's message. "What manner of man was he which came up to meet you, and told you these words?" the king enquired. "And they answered him, He was a hairy man, and girt with a girdle of leather about his loins. And he said, It is Elijah the Tishbite." In his perverse folly, Ahaziah ordered at once that the prophet be apprehended. But now the strong hand of Jehovah must be felt by the perverse king and his haughty captains: twice the captains with their fifty men are consumed by fire from heaven. But, as the third captain humbly pleads for his own life and the lives of his men sent out to arrest Jehovah's prophet, the angel of the Lord bids Elijah, "Go down with him: be not afraid of him. And he arose, and went down with him unto the king." There, in the presence of the king, Jehovah's judgment is unflinchingly repeated to him.

"So he died according to the word of the Lord which Elijah had spoken. And Jehoram reigned in his stead in the second year of Jehoram the son of Jehoshaphat king of Judah; because he had no son." This Jehoram, also known as Joram, was another son of Ahab (2 Kings 3:1) and therefore brother of Ahaziah.

"Now the rest of the acts of Ahaziah which he did, are they not written in the book of the chronicles of the kings of Israel?" Yes, and they, with the wicked acts recorded here, are written in God's books above, as well as all the deeds and doings of every man's life, whether it be good or evil. Solemn facts for us all!

JORAM
(or JEHORAM)

Exalted by Jehovah
(2 Kings 1:17; 3:1–27; 6:8–7:20; 9:1–26)

Contemporary Prophet: Elisha

The wicked are overthrown, and are not: but the house of the righteous shall stand.

Proverbs 12:7

ow Jehoram the son of Ahab began to reign over Israel in Samaria the eighteenth year of Jehoshaphat king of Judah, and reigned twelve years. And he wrought evil in the sight of the Lord; but not like his father, and like his mother"—in contrast with his late brother Ahaziah, see 1 Kings 22:52—"for he put away the image of Baal that his father had made. Nevertheless he cleaved unto the sins of Jeroboam the son of Nebat, which made Israel to sin; he departed not therefrom" (2 Kings 3:1–3). There is no discrepancy between "the eighteenth year of Jehoshaphat," and "the second year of Jehoram the son of Jehoshaphat" (2 Kings 1:17). Jehoshaphat made his son joint-king a number of years before his death, (see 2 Kings 8:16) which readily accounts for the seeming contradictions in the above noted passages.

Moab had been tributary to Israel ever since their subjugation by David, more than two hundred years before (see 2 Samuel 8:2). On the division of the kingdom, they appear to have paid their accustomed tribute to Jeroboam, as his kingdom embraced the two and a half tribes east of Jordan, whose territory extended to the kingdom of Moab. "And Mesha king of Moab was a sheep master, and rendered unto the king of Israel a hundred thousand lambs, and a hundred thousand rams, with the wool. But it came to pass, when Ahab was dead, that the king of Moab rebelled against the king of Israel" (2 Kings 3:4–5). The defeat of the allied forces of Israel and Judah at Ramoth-gilead, probably emboldened him to take this step. This revolt of Mesha is mentioned on the Moabite, or Dibon, stone (see also Isaiah 16:1). The loss of this enormous annual income must have been keenly felt by Israel, and the attempt to secure its resumption occasioned this unhappy war in which Jehoshaphat, the king of Judah, foolishly allied himself to Jehoram.

> And king Jehoram went out of Samaria the same time, and numbered all Israel. And he went and sent to Jehoshaphat the king of Judah, saying, The king of Moab hath rebelled against me: wilt thou go with me against Moab to battle? And he said, I will go up: I am as thou art, my people as thy people, and my horses as thy horses.

This was a sadly compromising declaration to come from the lips of Jehoshaphat, a king of the house and lineage of David. But it was the result of his affinity with the house of Ahab by his son Jehoram's marriage to the infamous Athaliah. So not only do "evil communications corrupt good manners," but also that delicate sense of truthful consistency, so evidently lacking in Jehoshaphat here.

The king of Edom who allied with them was not a native Edomite, but a deputy (1 Kings 22:47) probably appointed by Jehoshaphat (2 Kings 8:20). He formed a party to the expedition in the capacity of a servant, rather than as an independent prince. "And they fetched a compass of seven days' journey: and there was no water for the host and for the cattle that followed them. And the king of Israel said, Alas! that the Lord hath called these three kings together to deliver them into the hand of Moab." When a man of God such as Jehoshaphat identifies himself with a man such as the king of Israel, distress must come upon them, that victory may be recognized as an act of God's sovereign grace, and not a spark of honor left to the follower of Jeroboam's calves.

"But Jehoshaphat said, Is there not here a prophet of the Lord, that we may enquire of the Lord by him?" Elisha is here, said one of the king of Israel's servants. "And Jehoshaphat said, The word of the Lord is with him. So the king of Israel, and Jehoshaphat, and the king of Edom went down to him." Even wicked men will cry to God in the hour of their calamity, yet without change of heart. But Elisha had as little respect for or fear of Jehoram, as Elijah his master had had for his idolatrous predecessors.

> And Elisha said unto the king of Israel, What have I to do with thee? get thee to the prophets of thy father, and to the prophets of thy mother. And the king of Israel said unto him,

Nay: for the Lord hath called these three kings together, to deliver them into the hand of Moab. And Elisha said, As the Lord of hosts liveth, before whom I stand, surely, were it not that I regard the presence of Jehoshaphat the king of Judah, I would not look toward thee, nor see thee (2 Kings 3:13–14).

Then, as the minstrel played, "the hand of the Lord came upon him," and he ordered the valley to be filled with ditches, saying, "Thus saith the Lord, Ye shall not see wind, neither shall ye see rain: yet that valley shall be filled with water, that ye may drink, both ye, and your cattle, and your beasts. And this is but a light thing in the sight of the Lord: He will deliver the Moabites also into your hand." And so, "It came to pass, in the morning, when the meat offering was offered, that, behold, there came water by the way of Edom, and the country was filled with water."

It has been suggested that this sudden and abundant water supply was caused by heavy rains on the eastern mountains of Edom, so far away that no signs of the storm were visible to the invaders. In any case it was God's doing, whatever the physical forces used by Him to bring it about. Faith never concerns itself with the scientific explanation of such occurrences. God could have created the water, had He so ordained. And "he giveth not account of any of his matters," either to adoring, wondering faith, or critical, questioning unbelief (Job 33:13). A starving man need not concern himself as to how or where the food set before him was obtained by his benefactor. It is his to eat, and be thankful. And anyone who hears of this benevolence should not be occupied with questions concerning the manner or means by which the philanthropist was enabled to do the beggar this kindness. His business should be to admire and laud the spirit of selfless love and mercy that prompted the deed of generosity.

"And when all the Moabites heard that the kings were come up to fight against them, they gathered all that were able to put on armor, and upward, and stood in the border." When the morning dawned they saw the water as the sun shone upon it in the ditches, and it appeared to them red as blood. "And they said, This is blood: the kings are surely slain, and they have smitten one another; now therefore, Moab, to the spoil." They probably supposed that the Edomites had turned mutinous, and in their effort to free themselves of Hebrew domination, had caused the mutual destruction of the confederate armies. But when they approached the Israelite camp, "The Israelites rose up and smote the Moabites, so that they fled before them." Their defeat was thorough, crushing, and unexpected. Israel seems now to have exceeded in unmerciful pursuit and pressure on the king of Moab, who in desperation "took his eldest son that should have reigned in his stead, and offered him for a burnt offering upon the wall. And there was great indignation against Israel: and they departed from him, and returned to their own land."

This was Jehoshaphat's second act of affinity with the ungodly, and like the first, it ended in failure, or was entirely barren of results (2 Chronicles 18). If even sinners wish success in their undertakings they should be careful not to admit into their partnership God's children, for God's hand may be on His children for discipline, and ill fortune will attend them. Neither Ahab, nor Jehoram gained anything by having the godly Jehoshaphat as their ally—so jealous is God of His people's associations.

How strange, yet sadly true, that the history of a country is largely the history of its wars. This maxim is true, not only of the land of Israel, but of its kings especially. Omit the records of their warfare and there would be little to say of any of them. How it all tells of man's fall and ruin, and of God's righteous government.

The second important incident recorded of Jehoram's life is in connection with the invasion of his territory by the king of Syria.

> Then the king of Syria warred against Israel, and took counsel with his servants, saying, In such and such a place shall be my camp. And the man of God sent unto the king of Israel, saying, Beware that thou pass not such a place; for thither the Syrians are come down. And the king of Israel sent to the place which the man of God told him and warned him of, and saved himself there, not once nor twice (2 Kings 6:8–10).

The prophet seems to look upon Jehoram here with somewhat less disfavor than when on the expedition against the Moabites (see also 2 Kings 3:13). He seems to have been pursued by the king of Syria, and there may have been some change in his conduct too, which Elisha would be quick to notice and encourage in every possible way—so gracious is God in His governmental dealings with the sons of men.

On learning how Jehoram obtained the information by which he was enabled to repeatedly escape the ambushments set for him, the king of Syria sent to apprehend the revealer of his military secrets. In answer to the prophet's prayer, the Lord blinded the Syrians, and the man they were bent on arresting led them into the very midst of their enemy's capital. "And the king of Israel said unto Elisha, when he saw them, My father, shall I smite them? shall I smite them?" But, in New Testament spirit, he answered,

> Thou shalt not smite them; wouldest thou smite those whom thou hast taken captive with thy sword and with thy bow? Set

bread and water before them, that they may eat and drink, and go to their master. And he prepared great provision for them: and when they had eaten and drunk, he sent them away, and they went to their master (2 Kings 6:22–23).

The Syrians had heard before that the kings of Israel were merciful kings (1 Kings 20:31); they were now given a demonstration of the mercy of Israel's God through His prophet's intervention. And it was not without some effect, for we read, "So the bands of Syria came no more into the land of Israel." Such is the power of grace, even over hardened, heathen soldiers.

"And it came to pass after this, that Ben-hadad king of Syria gathered all his host, and went up, and besieged Samaria." This does not in any way contradict what is stated in the preceding verse (2 Kings 6:23–24). Josephus wrote, "So he [Ben-hadad] determined to make no more *secret* attempts upon the king of Israel" (*Antiquities* 9.4.4). He afterwards made open war upon him, by legitimate methods; no more by marauding bodies and ambushments.

Sadly, Israel's heart was so hardened that in the famine accompanying the siege, instead of turning to Jehovah, some of the inhabitants in their terrible extremity turned to the horrible deed of eating even their own offspring! (see Leviticus 26:26–29; Deuteronomy 28:52–53; which was finally fulfilled under the Romans). "And as the king of Israel was passing by upon the wall, there cried a woman unto him, saying, Help, my lord, O king. And he said, If the Lord do not help thee, whence shall I help thee? out of the barnfloor, or out of the winepress? And the king said unto her, What aileth thee?" (2 Kings 6:26–28) And then he was told the terrible tale of women deliberately agreeing to boil and eat their own children!

> And it came to pass, when the king heard the words of the
> woman, that he rent his clothes; and he passed by upon the
> wall, and the people looked, and, behold, he had sackcloth
> within upon his flesh. Then he said, God do so and more also
> to me, if the head of Elisha the son of Shaphat shall stand on
> him this day.

He had sackcloth on his flesh, but murder in his heart.
What power of Satan over man's heart and mind is revealed
in this! The heart of the king rose in bitter passion against
God, and His prophet would serve to vent the rage of his un-
repentant, unsubdued heart. It is not the only occasion in
history where rulers have blamed God for national calami-
ties. How often men's hearts rise against God, rather than
humble themselves in repentance, under the pains of what
they cannot change or overcome (see Revelation 16:10–11).

The king therefore sent an executioner to carry out his
hasty threat. His motive in following after his executioner is
not clear. Was it to see the accomplishment of his murderous
design, or regret at his reckless order?

> But Elisha sat in his house, and the elders sat with him; and the
> king sent a man from before him: but ere the messenger came
> to him, he said to the elders, See ye how this son of a murderer
> hath sent to take away my head? Look, when the messenger
> cometh, shut the door, and hold him fast at the door: is not the
> sound of his master's feet behind him? And while he yet talked
> with them, behold, the messenger came down unto him: and
> he [the king] said, Behold, this evil is of the Lord, what [why,
> N.Tr.] should I wait for the Lord any longer? (2 Kings
> 6:32–33)

He had professedly been waiting on the God of Elisha, and now when deliverance seemed far off, he throws all faith away, as if to say, It is useless to look to the Lord for deliverance; and the unbelief and passion of his heart break out.

But human extremity is the divine opportunity. When the unbelieving king broke out in fretful despair, the faith of God's prophet shined out, proclaiming full relief and abundance on the morrow. "Then Elisha said, Hear ye the word of the Lord; Thus saith the Lord, Tomorrow about this time shall a measure of fine flour be sold for a shekel, and two measures of barley for a shekel, in the gate of Samaria" (7:1). And as the man of God foretold, so it came to pass. A miraculous noise from the Lord frightened the besieging army, supposing it to be a mighty host's arrival.

> For the Lord had made the host of the Syrians to hear a noise of chariots, and a noise of horses, even the noise of a great host: and they said one to another, Lo, the king of Israel hath hired against us the kings of the Hittites, and the kings of the Egyptians, to come upon us. Wherefore they arose and fled in the twilight, and left their tents, and their horses, and their asses, even the camp as it was, and fled for their life (6–7).

Lepers, in the night brought the welcome news to the king, who delayed the deliverance by his unbelief, sending as far as the Jordan—a score of miles away—for proof of the report. Thus was Samaria relieved.

As for Syria, the dynasty of the first two Ben-hadads was soon after ended with the strangling of the king on his sickbed by his prime minister Hazael, who reigned in his stead (2 Kings 8:15). News of this revolution probably encouraged Jehoram to attempt the recovery of Ramoth-gilead, which his father, fourteen years before, had attacked in vain, with fatal consequences to himself. "And he [Jehoram, king of Judah] went with Joram the son of Ahab to the war against Hazael king of Syria in Ramoth-gilead; and the Syrians wounded Joram. And king Joram went back to be healed in Jezreel of the wounds which the Syrians had given him at Ramah [or Ramoth], when he fought against Hazael king of Syria" (28–29).

He was slain shortly after by Jehu his commander-in-chief. We will read more of this in the chapter of that king's life (see JEHU; also JEHORAM in *Kings of Judah*). The dynasty of Omri (the most powerful of the nine that ruled over Israel) ended with Joram. His character was neither strong, nor very marked in anything. He appears to have had leanings toward the worship of Jehovah, but as a patron rather than in heart-subjection to Him as the one true God of Heaven and earth. He evidently considered Elisha's miracles as matters of speculation, in idle curiosity inquiring of the prophet's disgraced servant Gehazi. "And the king talked with Gehazi the servant of the man of God, saying, Tell me, I pray thee, all the great things that Elisha hath done." These marvelous signs of Jehovah were to him merely material for entertainment, as the miracles of Elisha's great antitype (John the Baptist) were to Herod (see Mark 6:14,20; Luke 9:9; 23:8). He counseled Jehoram king of Judah to his destruction (2 Chronicles 22:4–5). Such was his unpopularity with his subjects that Jehu had little difficulty in effecting a revolution, and usurping his throne.

He appears to have been, in spiritual matters, one of those undecided, neutral characters who puzzle most observers, and who never seem to know themselves just where they stand or belong. He put away the Baal statue made by his father Ahab, but never became a real believer in Jehovah. The reading of the inspired record of his life leaves the impression on one's mind that he was, in all matters of faith, both skeptical and superstitious. God, who knew him and his ways perfectly, has caused it to be recorded of him, "He wrought evil in the sight of the Lord." As such, we and all posterity know him. And as such he will be revealed in the coming day, when great and small shall stand before the throne to be judged, "every man, according to his works."

JEHU

Jehovah is He
(2 Kings 9–10)

CONTEMPORARY PROPHET: Elisha

The great God that formed all things both rewardeth the fool, and rewardeth transgressors.
                                        Proverbs 26:10

*J*ehu had probably been anointed by Elijah twenty years before the recorded anointing in 2 Kings 9 (see 1 Kings 19:16). We remember that David was anointed by Samuel long before his anointing by the people (2 Samuel 2:4). Although some commentators feel that the anointing of Jehu was left to Elijah's successor, to be done at God's appointed time.

And Elisha the prophet called one of the children of the prophets, and said unto him, Gird up thy loins, and take this box of oil in thy hand, and go to Ramoth-gilead: and when thou comest thither, look out there Jehu the son of Jehoshaphat the son of Nimshi, and go in, and make him arise up from among his brethren, and carry him to an inner chamber; then take the box of oil, and pour it on his head, and say, Thus saith the Lord, I have anointed thee king over Israel. Then open the door, and flee, and tarry not.

The anointing of the king over Israel was not an established custom or rule. It was done when the circumstances were out of the ordinary, or when there might be some question as to his title to the crown. Saul and David were both anointed by Samuel; the one as *first* king, the other as head of a new line (1 Samuel 9:16; 16:12). Zadok the priest and Nathan the prophet jointly anointed Solomon, because of the faction under Adonijah (1 Kings 1:34). The rebel son Absalom was also anointed (2 Samuel 19:10); so was the boy-king Joash (2 Kings 11:12) and the wicked and ill-fated Jehoahaz (2 Kings 23:30). "In the case of Jehu, in whom the succession of the kingdom of Israel was to be translated out of the right line of the family of Ahab, into another family, which had no [legal] right to the kingdom, but merely the appointment of God, there was a necessity for his unction, both to convey to him a title, and to invest him in the actual possession of the kingdom" (Burder).

Joram's army still lay siege to Ramoth-gilead, where his general Jehu commanded the forces.

So the young man, even the young man the prophet, went to Ramoth-gilead....and he said, I have an errand unto thee, O captain....and he poured the oil on his head, and said unto him, Thus saith the Lord God of Israel, I have anointed thee king over the people of the Lord, even over Israel. And thou shalt smite the house of Ahab thy master, that I may avenge the blood of my servants the prophets, and the blood of all the servants of the Lord, at the hand of Jezebel. For the whole house of Ahab shall perish…and the dogs shall eat Jezebel in the portion of Jezreel, and there shall be none to bury her (2 Kings 9:4–10).

At last, after more than fifteen years' delay, the blood of Naboth, crying like Abel's for vengeance from the ground, was about to be requited. God, when judging men, is never in haste. He allowed Jezebel to outlive, not only her husband, but his two successors. She was powerless, evidently, to continue her former high-handed practices after Ahab's death; and it was a part of her punishment to live to see his dynasty overthrown and the beginning of the extinction of his and her house.

Then Jehu came forth to the servants of his Lord: and one said unto him, Is all well? wherefore came this mad fellow to thee? And he said unto them, Ye know the man, and his communication. And they said, It is false; tell us now. And he said, Thus and thus spake he to me, saying, Thus saith the Lord, I have anointed thee king over Israel. Then they hasted, and took every man his garment, and put it under him on the top of the stairs [an ancient custom, see Matthew 21:7], and blew with trumpets, saying, Jehu is king…And Jehu said, If it be your minds, then let none go forth nor escape out of the city to go to tell it in Jezreel (2 Kings 9:11–15).

Impatient to be in actual and acknowledged possession of the kingdom and without a thought of waiting on God, even for a brief season, Jehu is off with Bidkar his captain on his thirty-five mile journey to Jezreel (16–20). Eager to be at his work of destruction, the newly anointed executioner-king makes all speed, as if the solemn, fearful work of destruction to which he had been commissioned was to him an exciting pleasure. It should have been a painful task of stern necessity had Jehu been in true fellowship with God in his work of overthrow and retributive judgment on the house of Ahab. God has no pleasure in the death of the sinner. The taking of human life, whether done by divine appointment or otherwise, is one of the saddest and most solemn acts that it is possible for man to perform. Jehu's ready willingness betrayed how little his soul really understood the awful nature of his charge and the gravity of the guilt that had occasioned it.

> And Joram said, Make ready! And his chariot was made ready. And Joram king of Israel and Ahaziah king of Judah went out, each in his chariot, and they went out against [to meet, N.TR.] Jehu, and met him in the portion of Naboth the Jezreelite. And it came to pass, when Joram saw Jehu, that he said, Is it peace, Jehu? And he answered, What peace, so long as the whoredoms of thy mother Jezebel and her witchcrafts are so many? And Joram turned his hands, and fled, and said to Ahaziah, There is treachery, O Ahaziah. And Jehu drew a bow with his full strength, and smote Jehoram between his arms, and the arrow went out at his heart, and he sunk down in his chariot (21–24).

It was but the sudden beginning of a speedy end; for God makes "a short work" with men when He makes inquisition for apostasy and blood.

Then said Jehu to Bidkar his captain, Take up and cast him in the portion of the field of Naboth the Jezreelite: for remember how that, when I and thou rode together after Ahab his father, the Lord laid this burden upon him...Now therefore take and cast him into the plot of ground, according to the word of the Lord (25–26).

They slew Ahaziah king of Judah also, as he was seeking to escape.

Jezebel's turn comes next. Her innate vanity manifested itself up until the last. She probably knew her end had come; instead of preparing her soul, she adorned her body (soon to be eaten by dogs), that she might appear queenly and beautiful even in death. Her daring spirit, even with her last breath, taunted her slayer by reminding him of Zimri's end, who like Jehu (as she would make it appear), "slew his master." Darby's translation of 2 Kings 9:31 makes Jezebel say, "Is it peace, Zimri, murderer of his master?"

And he [Jehu] lifted up his face to the window, and said, Who is on my side? who? And there looked out to him two or three eunuchs. And he said, Throw her down. So they threw her down...And [he] said, Go, see now this cursed woman, and bury her: for she is a king's daughter. And they went to bury her: but they found no more of her than the skull, and the feet, and the palms of her hands. Wherefore they came again, and told him. And he said, This is the word of the Lord, which He spake by His servant Elijah the Tishbite, saying, In the portion of Jezreel shall dogs eat the flesh of Jezebel: and the carcass of Jezebel shall be as dung upon the face of the field in the portion of Jezreel; so that they shall not say, This is Jezebel (32–37).

God had decreed that no tomb should mark the resting place of her remains.

Thus miserably perished this wretched woman, a foreigner in Israel, who did her utmost to make her Tyrian Baal worship the established religion of her husband's kingdom, and hesitated not to slay any who dared oppose her propaganda, or interfere with her desires or designs in anyway. Her tragic death is as the shadow cast before of that coming event foretold in Revelation 17—Babylon's end, "the judgment of the great whore," whose idolatries and crimes have stained the earth.

Next we read of Jehu's letter to the caretakers of Ahab's seventy children (2 Kings 10:1–3). It was seemingly a bold challenge, though in reality only his manner of frightening them into subjection. He knew well the character of those with whom he had to deal; besides, there does not appear to have been much love or loyalty to the reigning dynasty. So the fervid reformer knew he had little to fear from them.

> But they were exceedingly afraid, and said, Behold, the two kings stood not before him: how then shall we stand? And he that was over the house, and he that was over the city, the elders also, and the bringers up of the children, sent to Jehu, saying, We are thy servants, and will do all that thou shalt bid us; we will not make any king: do thou that which is good in thine eyes (4–5).

These spiritless elders and rulers of Jezreel tamely surrendered everything to Jehu. When Jezebel sent her imperious letter to them, commanding them to falsely accuse and then murder Naboth, they abjectly complied without the slightest show of resistance or conscience, putting to death their righteous fellow townsman. Jehu might well have expected a cringing obedience from such men.

Then he wrote a letter the second time to them, saying, If ye
be mine, and if ye will hearken unto my voice, take ye the
heads of the men your master's sons, and come to me to
Jezreel by tomorrow this time....And it came to pass, when
the letter came to them, that they took the king's sons, and
slew seventy persons, and put their heads in baskets, and sent
him them in Jezreel....And it come to pass in the morning,
that he went out, and stood, and said to all the people, Ye be
righteous: behold, I conspired against my master, and slew
him: but who slew all these? (6–9)

It was a crafty stroke of policy on Jehu's part to have the
principal men of the capital slay the residue of Ahab's posterity. He shrewdly determined that their act would create a
breach between themselves and any sympathizers with the
extinct dynasty, or their royal relatives across the border. Thus
the last remaining opposition to his course and settlement on
the throne was effectively destroyed.

Though his motives were purely political, he gave his
wholesale executions a religious coloring by reminding the
people of God's word and principle of retribution in regard
to Ahab and his house:

Know now that there shall fall unto the earth nothing of the
word of the Lord, which the Lord spake concerning the house
of Ahab: for the Lord hath done that which he spake by his
servant Elijah. So Jehu slew all that remained of the house of
Ahab in Jezreel, and all his great men, and his kinsfolks, and his
priests, until he left him none remaining (10–11).

The sword of judgment, so far as the expressed purpose of
Jehovah was concerned, should have been confined to the
house of Ahab. But a reckless and ambitious hand was wielding

it, and it devoured beyond the allotted limits. It was not any part of Jehovah's commission to Jehu to slay the family of Ahaziah, or any of the descendants of king Jehoshaphat. God had not required this at his hands; and in his unwarranted slaughter of these brethren of Ahaziah he all but exterminated the house of David, leaving the rule of the kingdom to the infamous Athaliah. Jehu evidently cared little for this. His thought was probably to prevent any uprising against himself from the royal family of Judah. The possible consequences of his ruthless act in reference to the continuance of David's line (until Messiah) gave him no concern. As to the butchered princes, they reaped the melancholy consequences of their intimacy with a family doomed by God to destruction for their apostasy and wickedness. Let Christians take warning and obey the call of God, which is so unmistakably imperative and plain, "Come out from among them, and be ye separate" (2 Corinthians 6:17).

Jehu's self-complacency is revealed in his meeting with Jehonadab the son of Rechab (2 Kings 10:15–17). He patronizingly took him into his chariot, giving him his hand (signifying a pledge, in the East; see Ezra 10:19), and saying, "Come with me, and see my zeal for the Lord." His ostentatious display of his reforming zeal revealed how little he had God's glory in mind in all his feverish activity and abolition—in sad contrast to Jesus who always hid Himself and sought His Father's glory only. He too had a zeal; but of what a different character from that of Jehu! "The zeal of thine house hath [consumed] me," He could say (John 2:17). But Jehu's zeal, on the contrary, consumed and destroyed everybody and everything that stood in the way of his own advantage or aggrandizement, but never touched himself. He appears to have been a total stranger to real exercise of soul. God ordained him as His executioner, and, as has been aptly said, "Never was a more fitted instrument for the work whereunto he was appointed than Jehu." He had his reward, and it was for this world alone; the fourth generation of his children saw its end.

"And when he was come to Samaria, he slew all that remained unto Ahab in Samaria, till he had destroyed him, according to the saying of the Lord, which he spake by Elijah." He then turned his attention to the priests of Baal. A monk, at the dawn of the Reformation, remarked, "We must root printing out, or it will root us out." Jehu felt the same toward the Baal worship in his newly-acquired kingdom; hence it must be rooted out. Baal had formed a powerful link between Ahab's family and his worshipers, and might be a menace to his tenure of the throne; his priests must therefore share the fate of that family under whose powerful patronage they had flourished in the past thirty-six years. "And Jehu gathered all the people together, and said unto them, Ahab served Baal a little; but Jehu shall serve him much." He then deceitfully gathered all the priests and followers of Baal into their place of worship. There is a measure of righteousness in his doings, however, for he takes pains to have none of the servants of Jehovah mixed up with the devoted worshipers of Baal.

> And it came to pass, as soon as he [they, N.TR.] had made an end of offering the burnt offering, that Jehu said to the guard and to the captains, Go in, and slay them; let none come forth. And they smote them with the edge of the sword; and the guard and the captains cast them out, and went to the city [some manuscripts read buildings or citadel] of the house of Baal. And they brought forth the images out of the house of Baal, and burned them. And they brake down the image of Baal, and brake down the house of Baal, and made it a draught house unto this day (2 Kings 10:25–27).

While he is God's faithful, and over-zealous instrument, there is nothing lovely, and little that is commendable, in the character of Jehu. "But Jehu took no heed to walk in the law of [Jehovah] the God of Israel with all his heart: for he departed not from the sins of Jeroboam, which made Israel to sin" (2 Kings 10:31). He served God's purpose as an executioner, but with that he stopped. He could slay "with all his heart," but took no heed to walk in the law of the Lord with earnestness. He could break down the gross and vile worship of Baal, yet continue in the calf worship of Jeroboam. It is easier to serve God in outward things than to acquire the character that He loves, enthroning Him in mind and heart. How different was David from Jehu! He too was God's instrument for judgment, but how different was his way of carrying it out. God did not, nor did He let Israel, forget Jehu's heartless slaughter, saying to the prophet Hosea, a hundred years later, "Call his name Jezreel; for yet a little while, and I will avenge the blood of Jezreel upon the house of Jehu" (Hosea 1:4).

The great lesson the servants of God can draw from this remarkable man's life is that of being constantly on our guard. We must not be found doing His work—either through discipline or evangelism—in a spirit of unbrokenness and without due exercise of heart and conscience before Him who is a God of judgment, and by whom actions are weighed.

Now the rest of the acts of Jehu, and all that he did, and all his might, are they not written in the book of the chronicles of the kings of Israel? And Jehu slept with his fathers: and they buried him in Samaria. And Jehoahaz his son reigned in his stead. And the time that Jehu reigned over Israel in Samaria was twenty and eight years (2 Kings 10:34–36).

JEHOAHAZ

Jehovah-seized
(2 King 13:1–9)

<small>CONTEMPORARY PROPHETS:</small> Elisha, and Jonah

When the righteous are in authority, the people rejoice: but when
the wicked beareth rule, the people mourn.
Proverbs 29:2

In describing the reign of Jehoahaz, the Bible gives no
variation from the same sorrowful formula usually used in describing the moral conduct of these Israelitish kings: "He did
that which was evil in the sight of the Lord." His ways may not
have appeared sinful in the sight of his fellows; but God, who
"seeth not as man seeth," pronounced it "evil," and sent on him
and his subjects the chastisement their wicked idolatry deserved.

"And the anger of the Lord was kindled against Israel, and He delivered them into the hand of Hazael king of Syria, and into the hand of Ben-hadad the son of Hazael, all their days." Hazael's conquest of the kingdom had begun in the days of Jehu, Jehoahaz' father: "In those days the Lord began to cut Israel short: and Hazael smote them in all the coasts of Israel; From Jordan eastward, all the land of Gilead, the Gadites, and the Reubenites, and the Manassites, from Aroer, which is by the river Arnon, even Gilead and Bashan" (2 Kings 10:32–33). Jehu, though so "swift to shed blood" in the beginning of his reign, was more slow to take the sword in defense of the land and people of God toward the end. Men of this class are seldom really good soldiers. They may be exceedingly active in obtaining the position they love and covet, while very careless about the true interests of the people of God. There is no hint that Jehu made the slightest attempt to resist these inroads of the king of Syria in his dominion. He probably remained timorously passive at Samaria while the encroachments on God's territory were being made. The Black Obelisk records that he ("Jahua") sent gold and silver to Shalmaneser I at this time, probably to invoke the Assyrian's aid against Hazael. Certainly valor was not characteristic of Jehu. Impetuosity is not courage, nor must we mistake enthusiasm for the earnestness of conviction. To boast when putting on the armor is an easy matter; the wise will wait until the time to take it off (1 Kings 20:11). Even then the truly wise will glory only in the Lord.

And Jehoahaz besought the Lord, and the Lord hearkened unto him: for he saw the oppression of Israel, because the king of Syria oppressed them. (And the Lord gave Israel a saviour, so that they went out from under the hand of the Syrians: and the children of Israel dwelt in their tents, as beforetime. Nevertheless they departed not from the sins of the house of Jeroboam, who made Israel to sin, but walked therein: and there remained the grove [Asherah, N.TR.] also in Samaria) (2 Kings 13:4–6).

In this parenthetic paragraph we see how Elisha's prophecy of Hazael's pitiless oppression of the children of Israel was fulfilled (2 Kings 8:11–13). Well might the man of God, who so dearly loved Israel, weep as before him stood the destined perpetrator of these cruelties against his people. Through these afflictions, God was seeking to turn them back to repentance from their idolatries. This bitter chastisement appears to have had a salutary effect on Jehoahaz, for he "besought Jehovah." When the goodness of God fails to bring men to repentance, His severity is required, and used (see Psalm 78:34; Hosea 5:15). "Accordingly God accepted of his repentance instead of virtue," Josephus wrote, "and, being desirous rather to admonish those that might repent, and not to determine that they should be utterly destroyed, he granted him deliverance from war and dangers. So the country having obtained peace, returned to its former condition, and flourished as before" (*Antiquities* 9.8.5).

Second Kings 13:4–6 seems to imply a temporary deliverance under the reign of Jehoahaz. This restoration to prosperity began in its fullness under Joash son of Jehoahaz (2 Kings 13:25), and culminated during the reign of his grandson Jeroboam II (2 Kings 14:25). Prayer is frequently answered after the petitioner has passed away. So let none say, like the wicked of old, in reference to God, "What profit should we have, if we pray unto him?" (Job 21:15) What profit? Ah, true prayer is always heard at the throne: "Whatsoever we ask, we know that we have the petitions that we desired of him" (1 John 5:15).

"Hazael king of Syria oppressed Israel all the days of Jehoahaz" (2 Kings 13:22). There was no respite until Joash's day. This must have been a test to Jehoahaz' faith, if his repentance was really the result of godly sorrow for his and the nation's sins. But when has untried faith ever flourished? Stagger not, then, nor stumble, beloved fellow believer, at "the trial of your faith." God heard Jehoahaz, though he died with Hazael busy at his work of devastation in his realm. "Neither did he leave of the people to Jehoahaz but fifty horsemen, and ten chariots, and ten thousand footmen; for the king of Syria had destroyed them, and had made them like the dust by threshing" (see Amos 1:3).

"Now the rest of the acts of Jehoahaz, and all that he did, and his might, are they not written in the book of the chronicles of the kings of Israel? And Jehoahaz slept with his fathers; and they buried him in Samaria: and Joash his son reigned in his stead."

JOASH
(or JEHOASH)

Jehovah-gifted
(2 Kings 13:10–25; 14:8–16)

CONTEMPORARY PROPHET: Jonah (?)

A man shall not be established by wickedness: but the root of the righteous shall not be moved.
                    Proverbs 12:3

I n the thirty and seventh year of Joash king of Judah began Jehoash the son of Jehoahaz to reign over Israel in Samaria, and reigned sixteen years" (2 Kings 13:10). It is evident from a comparison of the figures of this verse with those given in verse 1 of the same chapter, and 14:1, that Joash (Jehoash, abbreviated) reigned jointly with his father during the last two years of the latter's life. This was not an uncommon custom in ancient times and readily explains an otherwise inexplicable chronological difficulty. It is quite likely that the seeming discrepancies of chronology in Scripture (those most difficult to solve) could be as simply and as satisfactorily explained. There may, of course, be a few which owe their origin to errors of transcription.

"And he did that which was evil in the sight of the Lord; he departed not from all the sins of Jeroboam the son of Nebat, who made Israel to sin: but he walked therein." Josephus called him a "good man" (*Antiquities* 9.8.6). This misjudgment of the character of Joash is probably based on the incident of his visit to the dying prophet Elisha (2 Kings 13:14–19). A little exhibition of religious, or even semi-religious, sentiment goes a long way with some persons in accounting people "good." Or Josephus may have been referring to the latter period of Joash's reign. It has been supposed by some that Joash reformed or repented toward the end of his life (perhaps founded partly on his mild treatment of Amaziah, when he had it in his power to take that combative meddler's life—see AMAZIAH in *Kings of Judah*). But the words, "He departed not from the sins of Jeroboam," forbid all thought of any real or lasting repentance at any period of his life. God is more anxious to record, than any of His people are to read, any good in any of these monarchs' lives. He has noted none in Joash's; and where He is silent, who will dare to speak?

The episode of Joash's visit to the dying prophet is simple to understand. Joash could not but realize that the prophet's departure from them would be a serious loss to the nation. In calling him "the chariot of Israel, and the horsemen thereof," he meant that the prophet's presence in their midst was to them what chariots and horsemen were to other nations— their main defense. And by placing his dying hands on those of the king, Elisha meant him to understand the truth of what God said more than three hundred years later, through the prophet Zechariah, "Not by might [or forces, or army], nor by power, but by my Spirit, saith the Lord of hosts" (Zechariah 4:6). "Without me, ye can do nothing," this would be in New Testament phraseology. The shooting of the arrow eastward, toward the territory conquered by Syria, signified Joash's victory over Ben-hadad's forces at Aphek ("on the road from Syria to Israel in the level plain east of Jordan; a common field of battles with Syria"—*Fausset*) (see 1 Kings 20:26). Only Joash's lack of faith, manifested in his halfhearted smiting the ground with arrows just three times, prevented his destroying the Syrians utterly. And it was unto him according to his faith. "And Jehoash the son of Jehoahaz took again out of the hand of Ben-hadad the son of Hazael the cities which he had taken out of the hand of Jehoahaz his father by war. *Three times* did Joash beat him, and recovered the cities of Israel" (2 Kings 13:25, italics added).

Like Asa, he had the opportunity given him to end the power of Syria (2 Chronicles 16:7), which from its beginning had been such a plague to both Judah and Israel. But, like Asa, he let it pass, and the work was left to the Assyrian, who destroyed both it (Syria) and them (Israel and Judah).

> And the rest of the acts of Joash, and all that he did, and his might wherewith he fought against Amaziah king of Judah, are they not written in the book of the chronicles of the kings of Israel? And Joash slept with his fathers, and was buried in Samaria with the kings of Israel; and Jeroboam his son reigned in his stead (2 Kings 14:15–16).

JEROBOAM II

Whose people is many
(2 Kings 14:23–29)

<small>CONTEMPORARY PROPHETS:</small> Hosea, and Amos

The froward is abomination to the Lord: but his secret is with the righteous.

Proverbs 3:32

*T*he reign of Jeroboam II was the longest and most prosperous of any of the reigns of the kings of Israel.

In the fifteenth year of Amaziah the son of Joash king of Judah, Jeroboam the son of Joash king of Israel began to reign in Samaria, and reigned forty and one years. And he did that which was evil in the sight of the Lord…He restored the coast of Israel from the entering of Hamath unto the sea of the plain, according to the word of the Lord God of Israel, which he spake by the hand of his servant Jonah, the son of Amittai, the prophet, which was of Gath-hepher.

This was the beginning of the ministry of the sixteen prophets whose writings have been preserved to us. Jonah was the earliest of these probably, and appears to have been Elisha's immediate successor. His prophecy referred to here, of the enlargement of Israel's coast (border), must have been a very pleasant one to him—a much more welcome work than his commission toward the Ninevites. But God's servants have no choice. They know the love of Christ and, constrained by that same love, it is their joy to tell it. But they also know the terror of the Lord, therefore they do their utmost to persuade and warn men of "the wrath to come." It is not grace only that came by Jesus Christ, but grace *and truth*. And the truth must be made known to men, however unpleasant or unthankful the task. But if done as unto God, it can never be a disagreeable or unwelcome undertaking to the spirit, however painful or unpleasant to the flesh (see 1 Corinthians 9:16–17).

The increase of Israel's territory under Jeroboam II was considerable; his prosperity in this way corresponding with his name—"whose people is many." "'The entering in of Hamath' indicates that the long valley between Lebanon and Anti-lebanon was the point of entrance into the land of Israel for an invading army" (Fausset). "The sea of the plain" was the Dead Sea (Joshua 3:16), making the total distance of his kingdom from north to south almost two hundred miles. He was, no doubt, the deliverer promised under the unfortunate reign of Jehoahaz (2 Kings 13:5). "For the Lord saw the affliction of Israel, that it was very bitter: for there was not any shut up, nor any left, nor any helper for Israel. And the Lord said not that he would blot out the name of Israel from under heaven: but he saved them by the hand of Jeroboam the son of Joash" (2 Kings 14:26–27). This was not for any goodness that He saw in them or Jeroboam their king, but because of His covenant with Abraham, Isaac, and Jacob (2 Kings 13:23).

"Now the rest of the acts of Jeroboam, and all that he did, and his might, how he warred, and how he recovered Damascus, and Hamath, which belonged to Judah, for Israel, are they not written in the book of the chronicles of the kings of Israel?" Damascus and Hamath were both capitals of two once powerful kingdoms, and though once subjugated by David (1 Chronicles 18:3–6), their recovery to Israel under Jeroboam, more than one hundred and fifty years after their revolt from Judah, speaks eloquently for the success and power of his armies against those hostile nations on his northern border. Hamath, called "the great" in Amos 6:2, was the principal city of upper Syria, and an important strategic point, commanding the whole valley of the Orontes leading to the countries on the south.

Israel was blessed with the ministries of both Hosea and Amos during Jeroboam's reign. From their writings it will readily be seen that though there was political revival under his rule, there was no real moral or spiritual awakening among the people. Amos was considered a troubler to the peace of the kingdom. He was admonished by Amaziah the priest of Bethel to flee away to the land of Judah, "and there eat bread, and prophesy there," as if God's prophet were nothing more than a mere mercenary like himself. He also accused the prophet before the king of having conspired against his life. Jeroboam appears to have paid little or no attention to this charge, being perhaps too sensible a man to believe the accusation, knowing the jealous, self-seeking spirit of the chief priest of the nation (see Amos 7:7–17).

"And Jeroboam slept with his fathers, even with the kings of Israel; and Zachariah his son reigned in his stead."

ZACHARIAH

Jah has remembered
(2 Kings 15:8–12)

Contemporary Prophet: Amos

Righteousness keepeth him that is upright in the way: but wickedness overthroweth the sinner.
Proverbs 13:6

There appears to be (from a comparison of dates) a period of about eleven years unaccounted for, between Jeroboam's death and the beginning of his son Zachariah's reign. This is not surprising when we see what quickly followed his accession to the throne.

In the thirty and eighth year of Azariah king of Judah did Zachariah the son of Jeroboam reign over Israel in Samaria six months. And he did that which was evil in the sight of the Lord, as his fathers had done: he departed not from the sins of Jeroboam the son of Nebat, who made Israel to sin. And Shallum the son of Jabesh conspired against him, and smote him before the people, and slew him, and reigned in his stead.

Anarchy probably prevailed during that unrecorded time. Hosea, whose prophecy dates about this time (as regards Israel, see Hosea 1:1), alluded frequently to this season of lawlessness and revolution. See Hosea 7:7; 10:3,7; 13:10—the last of these reads in the New Translation, "Where then is thy king?" The people were probably unwilling to have Zachariah succeed his father to the throne. He appears to have been quite unpopular with the mass of the nation, for Shallum slew him without fear *"before the people."* But God has said next to nothing as to this parenthetic period, and we dare not say more. To speculate here would be worse than folly, since God's wisdom has chosen to give us no record of it. Where no useful end is gained, He always hides from the gaze of the curious the sins and errors of His people.

The assassination of Zachariah ended the dynasty of Jehu, five generations in all, and extending over a period of more than a hundred years. But at last God avenged "the blood of Jezreel upon the house of Jehu" (Hosea 1:4). God's eyes were on the sinful kingdom (Amos 9:8), and its sinful kings. And from the time of Jeroboam's death, declension set in, ending less than seventy years later in its final overthrow and dissolution. Prophetic ministry was from this time greatly increased. "Such is the way of our gracious God," an unknown writer said, "that when judgment is near to approach, then testimony is multiplied." The prophecies of Hosea and

Amos abundantly testify as to how much God's word was needed in Israel.

> And the rest of the acts of Zachariah, behold, they are written in the book of the chronicles of the kings of Israel. This was the word of the Lord, which he spake unto Jehu, saying, Thy sons shall sit upon the throne of Israel unto the fourth generation. And so it came to pass.

And thus was it written by the prophet, "At daybreak shall the king of Israel utterly be cut off" (Hosea 10:15, N.TR.).

Zachariah's name—"Jah has remembered"—was strikingly significant. God did not forget the wholesale slaughter of men—many of them perhaps better than their executioner. Though a century had passed, *Jah* remembered and made the inevitable "inquisition for blood" on the fifth and final member of the murderer's succession.

SHALLUM

Requital
(2 Kings 15:13–15)

CONTEMPORARY PROPHET: Amos (?)

An evil man seeketh only rebellion: therefore a cruel messenger
shall be sent against him.

Proverbs 17:11

*S*hallum the son of Jabesh began to reign in the nine
and thirtieth year of Uzziah king of Judah; and he reigned a
full month in Samaria. For Menahem the son of Gadi went up
from Tirzah, and came to Samaria, and smote Shallum the
son of Jabesh in Samaria, and slew him, and reigned in his stead."
This assassin was not allowed to live long in his ill-gotten
power—only for a brief four weeks—and then met the just

reward of his crime. His name (a very common one in Israel) means "recompense" or "retribution"; as he requited his predecessor, so did Menahem his successor recompense him. It is the old principle of governmental just retribution exemplified.

This assassination of two rulers, Zachariah and Shallum, within the space of half a year, speaks loudly of the state of anarchy prevailing in the kingdom at the time. It was, as the prophet testified, "blood toucheth blood" (Hosea 4:2). The great prosperity and expansion under Jeroboam II appears to have corrupted the people and caused them to give free rein to their evil desires and violence (see Hosea 4:7).

Those in authority, instead of checking this spirit of lawlessness, found pleasure in it. "They make the king glad with their wickedness, and the princes with their lies" (Hosea 7:3). Excessive dissipation marked the conduct of these princes under this monarchy: "In the day of our king, the princes made themselves sick with the heat of wine" (Hosea 7:5, N.TR.). The demoralized condition of public affairs can scarcely be wondered at, when the king himself encouraged the disdain of the lawless: "He stretched out his hand to scorners." Disintegration and bloodshed followed as a natural consequence. Out of the political chaos and disorder following the death of Jeroboam II, Israel's most powerful king, came the undesired Zachariah, and his murderer Shallum. So wickedness brings its own reward, whether it be in a nation, a family, or an individual.

And the rest of the acts of Shallum, and his conspiracy which he made, behold, they are written in the book of the chronicles of the kings of Israel.

MENAHEM

Comforter
(2 Kings 15:16–22)

By the blessing of the upright the city is exalted: but it is overthrown by the mouth of the wicked.
Proverbs 11:11

Josephus asserted that Menahem was general of the Israelite forces. His coming up from Tirzah to slay Shallum, and
afterwards starting from Tirzah (where the main army was post-
ed) on his expedition of slaughter against Tiphsah, implies as
much. "Then Menahem smote Tiphsah, and all that were therein, and the coasts thereof from Tirzah: because they opened not
to him, therefore he smote it; and all the women therein that
were with child he ripped up." Tiphsah was originally one of
Solomon's northeastern border cities, on the Euphrates (1

Kings 4:24). It was doubtless recovered to Israel under Jeroboam II, and was probably in revolt when so cruelly attacked by the war-king Menahem. "Situated on the western bank of the Euphrates, on the great trade road from Egypt, Syria, and Phenicia to Mesopotamia, it was important for Menahem to rescue it" (Fausset). He, in all likelihood, expected by his brutal treatment of the Tiphsahites to strike terror to all who were likely to oppose his tenure of the crown.

> In the nine and thirtieth year of Azariah king of Judah began Menahem the son of Gadi to reign over Israel, and reigned ten years in Samaria. And he did that which was evil in the sight of the Lord: he departed not all his days from the sins of Jeroboam the son of Nebat, who made Israel to sin. And Pul the king of Assyria came against the land: and Menahem gave Pul a thousand talents of silver, that his hand might be with him to confirm the kingdom in his hand. And Menahem exacted the money of Israel, even of all the mighty men of wealth, of each man fifty shekels of silver, to give to the king of Assyria. So the king of Assyria turned back, and stayed not there in the land (2 Kings 15:17–20).

This is the first mention of the dreaded "Assyrian" in Scripture. Assyriologists are not perfectly agreed as to just who this *Pul* of Scripture was. The name (that form of it, at least) is not found on any of the Assyrian monuments. A *Phulukh* is mentioned in the Nimrud inscription, with whom some would identify him. Berosus mentioned a Chaldean king named Pul, who reigned at just this time, and where the wise cannot among themselves agree we must not venture even to put forth an opinion. Instead we pass on to that concerning which there can be no doubt—his invasion of the land, and the enormous price paid by Menahem for peace.

Some suppose that Pul regarded Menahem's reduction of Tiphsah as an attack on his territory; hence his march against his kingdom. But it is more probable that it was a mere plundering incursion, as most of these ancient military expeditions were, especially those of Assyria. The burden of the levy fell on the rich, which needs not excite much sympathy when we learn from the prophets Amos and Micah how their riches were obtained (see Amos 4:1; 5:11–12; 8:4–6; Micah 2:2; 6:10–12).

"And the rest of the acts of Menahem, and all that he did, are they not written in the book of the chronicles of the kings of Israel? And Menahem slept with his fathers; and Pekahiah his son reigned in his stead." Though he probably reigned as a military dictator merely, he evidently died in peace, as the expression "slept with his fathers" implies. The expression "his fathers" implies too that he was an Israelite, though his name *Menahem* does not sound like Hebrew. It is found nowhere else in Scripture, nor is that of his father (*Gadi,* "fortunate")—a peculiar and somewhat remarkable, if not significant, circumstance. A competent and spiritually-minded Semitic philologist would, we believe, find an ample and productive field for original research here, as well as in many other portions of Old Testament Scripture, especially the opening chapters of 1 Chronicles.

Menahem's name appears on the monuments of Tiglath-pileser, though it is thought by some, for various reasons, that the Assyrian chroniclers confused the name of Menahem with that of Pekah—his son's slayer. But this, like everything of merely human origin, is uncertain. Only in divinely inspired Scripture have we absolute exactitude and certainty; for He who was the Truth declared, "the Scripture cannot be broken." Hence they "are most surely believed among us" (Luke 1:1).

PEKAHIAH

Jah has observed
(2 Kings 15:23–26)

The righteousness of the upright shall deliver them: but transgressors shall be taken in their own naughtiness.
Proverbs 11:5

In the fiftieth year of Azariah king of Judah, Pekahiah the son of Menahem began to reign over Israel in Samaria, and reigned two years. And he did that which was evil in the sight of the Lord: he departed not from the sins of Jeroboam the son of Nebat, who made Israel to sin." Azariah (Uzziah), King of Judah, during his long reign of more than half a century, saw the death of five of Israel's kings, three of whom were assassinated, in addition to a period of anarchy lasting at least eleven years. This marked contrast between the two kingdoms is what the prophet probably referred to when he wrote, "Ephraim encompasseth me about with lies, and the house of Israel with deceit, but Judah yet walketh with God [El], and with the holy things of truth" (Hosea 11:12, N.TR.). This does not mean that all Judah's ways pleased the Lord, but that unlike apostate Israel, Judah maintained the truth of Jehovah as revealed in the law and symbolized in the temple's worship and service.

"But Pekah the son of Remaliah, a captain of his, conspired against him, and smote him in Samaria, in the palace of the king's house, with Argob and Arieh, and with him fifty men of the Gileadites: and he killed him, and reigned in his room." Pekahiah was assassinated by his captain (*shalish,* aide-de-camp, probably; "the general of his house," Josephus says) Pekah, with two of his followers, and a company of fifty Gileadites. Gilead was a direct descendant of Manasseh, oldest son of Joseph, and head of a large, powerful family, to whom Moses gave the conquered territory east of Jordan called Gilead (see Numbers 32:39–41; Deuteronomy 3:13; and Judges 12:4). These Gileadites appear to have been a rough, wild class, a kind of Hebrew highlanders, and ready in Pekahiah's day for any and all manner of villainy. See Hosea 6:8. They slew the king in his very palace ("with his friends at a feast;" Josephus *Antiquities* 9.11.1), so bold were they. *Pekahiah* means "Jah has observed" and implies that God had witnessed the murder of Shallum by Pekahiah's father Menahem, and had avenged that murder in the death of his son (2 Chronicles 24:22). His name, like his father's and grandfather's, does not occur anywhere else in Scripture.

"And the rest of the acts of Pekahiah, and all that he did, behold, they are written in the book of the chronicles of the kings of Israel." His death ended the seventh dynasty of the Israelitish kings.

PEKAH

Watch
(2 Kings 15:27–31)

Contemporary Prophet: Oded

As righteousness tendeth to life: so he that pursueth evil pursueth it to his own death.
Proverbs 11:19

n the two and fiftieth year of Azariah [Uzziah] king of Judah, Pekah the son of Remaliah began to reign over Israel in Samaria, and reigned twenty years. And he did that which was evil in the sight of the Lord: he departed not from the sins of Jeroboam the son of Nebat, who made Israel to sin." How painfully this oft-recurring testimony, like a sad refrain, falls on the ear! But this is the last time. Under Hoshea,

Pekah's slayer and successor, God made "to cease the kingdom of the house of Israel" (Hosea 1:4). And Hoshea, though he did evil, did it "not as the kings of Israel that were before him" (2 Kings 17:2).

"In the days of Pekah king of Israel came Tiglath-pileser king of Assyria, and took Ijon, and Abel-beth-maachah, and Janoah, and Kedesh, and Hazor, and Gilead, and Galilee, all the land of Naphtali, and carried them captive to Assyria." This occurred after Pekah's unprovoked and cowardly attack on Jerusalem, together with Rezin king of Damascus (see AHAZ in *Kings of Judah*). And the king of Assyria's invasion and devastation of his land was his just reward for his fierce anger and evil counsel against the house of David, which he sought to overthrow by conspiracy and revolution (see Isaiah 7:4–6).

Pekah slew one hundred thousand Jews in one day (2 Chronicles 28:5–6); and God requited him in kind. For as he had so treacherously shed man's blood, by man was his blood also treacherously shed. "And Hoshea the son of Elah made a conspiracy against Pekah the son of Remaliah, and smote him, and slew him, and reigned in his stead, in the twentieth year of Jotham the son of Uzziah."

Josephus wrote that Hoshea was a friend of Pekah's (*Antiquities* 9.13.1). In his death the prophecy of Isaiah 7:16 was fulfilled. His name, meaning "watch," is from a root, "to open" (as the eyes); figuratively, to "be observant" (Strong). But watch as he might, his very friend in whom he trusted became, in the ordering of God, his slayer; so impossible is it for the wicked to escape their merited retribution from the hand of Him who has said, "Vengeance is mine; I will repay" (read Amos 9:1–5).

"And the rest of the acts of Pekah, and all that he did, behold, they are written in the book of the chronicles of the kings of Israel."

HOSHEA

Deliverer
(2 Kings 15:30; 17:1–6)

Scornful men bring a city into a snare: but wise men turn away wrath.

Proverbs 29:8

n the twelfth year of Ahaz king of Judah began Hoshea the son of Elah to reign in Samaria over Israel nine years." He was the last of the nineteen kings who ruled (or, rather, misruled) Israel. A period of at least eight years (see HEZEKIAH in *Kings of Judah*) occurred between the murder of Pekah, Hoshea's predecessor, and his actual assumption of the throne. Why this kingless interval we have no means of knowing, nor how the time was occupied. Josephus, even if we could always trust him, gives us no help here (the usual way of rewriters or would-be improvers of Scripture history), for he passed the subject over in silence. It was probably a period of anarchy in the land, when Hosea's position was disputed.

But God's Word has chronicled Hoshea's wickedness thus: "And he did that which was evil in the sight of the Lord, but not as the kings of Israel that were before him." There is nothing in that sentence that could be construed to Hoshea's credit, for the Assyrian plunderers had in all probability removed and carried away the golden calves of Dan and Bethel (see Hosea 10:5–8). If he did not worship them, or other abominations, it was not because he abhorred idols.

But his evil doings, whatever their character, speedily brought the Assyrian—"the rod of God's anger"—upon him and his wicked subjects. "Against him came up Shalmaneser king of Assyria; and Hoshea became his servant, and gave him presents." He who conspired against his weaker Israelite master attempted the same (to his sorrow) with this powerful Gentile lord. "And the king of Assyria found conspiracy in Hoshea: for he had sent messengers to So king of Egypt, and brought no present to the king of Assyria, as he had done year by year: therefore the king of Assyria shut him up, and bound him in prison."

The siege of Samaria occurred before Hoshea's imprisonment, even though recorded after. "Hoshea's imprisonment was not *before* the capture of Samaria, but the sacred writer first records the *eventual* fate of Hoshea himself, then details the invasion as it affected Samaria and Israel" (Fausset).

> Then the king of Assyria came up throughout all the land, and went up to Samaria, and besieged it three years. In the ninth year of Hoshea the king of Assyria took Samaria, and carried Israel away into Assyria, and placed them in Halah and in Habor by the river of Gozan, and in the cities of the Medes (2 Kings 17:5–6).

This siege and capture of Samaria are recorded on the monuments of Assyria just as they are narrated in 2 Kings 17. What finally became of Hoshea is not revealed, unless he is the king meant in the prophet's poetic allusion, "As for Samaria, her king is cut off as the foam upon the water" (Hosea 10:7). His name means "deliverer," and may have a prophetic significance. It serves as a gracious reminder to the now long scattered nation, of that great Deliverer who will "come out of Zion and turn away ungodliness from Jacob." And then, "all Israel shall be saved" (Romans 11:26).

⋆　　　⋆　　　⋆

In 2 Kings 17:7–23 we are given an instructive and touching review of Israel's downward course. It has been truly observed that the most dismal picture of Old Testament history is that of the kingdom of Israel. Of the nine distinct dynasties that successively ruled the dissevered tribes, three ended with the total extermination of the reigning family. The kingdom lasted for a period of about 250 years, and the inspired records of those eventful two-and-a-half centuries of Israel's kings and people furnish us with little more than repeated and fearful exhibitions of lawlessness and evil. Out of the nineteen kings that ruled Israel from the great division to the deportation of the people to the land of Assyria, only seven died natural deaths (Baasha, Omri, Jehu, Jehoahaz, Jehoash, Jeroboam II, and Menahem); seven were assassinated (Nadab, Elah, Joram, Zachariah, Shallum, Pekaiah, and Pekah); one committed suicide (Zimri); one died of wounds received in battle (Ahab); one was "struck" by the judgment of God (Jeroboam); one died of injuries received from a fall (Ahaziah); and the other, and last (Hoshea), apparently was "cut off as foam upon the water." To this meaningful array of facts must be added two prolonged periods of anarchy, when there was no king in Israel, every man doing, in all likelihood, "that which was right in his own eyes."

The kingdom of Judah continued for more than a century and a quarter after the kingdom of Israel had ceased to exist, making its history fully one-third longer than that of the ten tribes. Then it too, like its sister-kingdom, fell into disintegration and decay, and was given up to the first universal empire under the renowned Nebuchadnezzar (see 2 Kings 25, and 2 Chronicles 36:15–23). This world monarchy began the "times of the Gentiles," during which "the most High ruleth [over] the kingdom of men, and giveth it to whomsoever he will" (Daniel 4:25)—setting up over it, at times, even the basest of men (as Belshazzar, the last Darius, Alexander, Nero, etc.). Since that day empire has superseded empire, dynasty has supplanted dynasty, and king succeeded king, as God has said, "I will overturn, overturn, overturn, it: and it shall be no more, until he come whose right it is; and I will give it him" (Ezekiel 21:27). We hope His coming will be very soon, and then the eye of weeping, waiting Israel "shall see the King in His beauty."

But before this, "the willful king," the "profane, wicked prince of Israel" (the antichrist) must come. And from his unworthy head shall be removed the crown (see Ezekiel 21:25–26), to be placed, with many others, on the once thorn-crowned brow of Him who is the King of kings and Lord of lords. That will be our highest joy and glory, to see Him, our Lord and Savior Jesus Christ honored and declared by all, as God's "firstborn, higher than the kings of the earth" (Psalm 89:27).

> *The Ruler over men shall be just,*
> *Ruling in the fear of God;*

And He shall be as the light of the morning,
Like the rising of the sun,
A morning without clouds,
When, from the sunshine after rain,
The green grass springeth from the earth.

. . . .

For this is all my salvation, And every desire
(2 Samuel 23:3–5, N. TR.).

"Amen. Even so, come, Lord Jesus."

BIBLIOGRAPHY

he author gratefully acknowledges the help of the following sources:

Darby, John Nelson. *Translation of the Old Testament.*

Fausset, Andrew Robert. *Bible Cyclopedia.*

Josephus, Flavius. *The Works of Josephus,* translated by William Whiston.

Strong, James. *Exhaustive Concordance of the Bible.*

OTHER READING:

Thiele, E. R. *The Mysterious Numbers of the Hebrew Kings.*

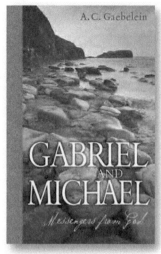
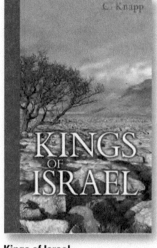
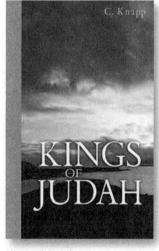
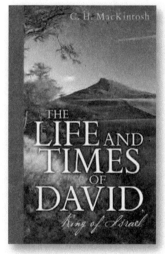